Higher Ed, Inc.

THE JOHNS HOPKINS UNIVERSITY PRESS

Higher Ed, Inc.

The Rise of the For-Profit University

Richard S. Ruch

The Johns Hopkins University Press

BALTIMORE AND LONDON

© 2001 The Johns Hopkins University Press
All rights reserved. Published 2001
Printed in the United States of America on acid-free paper

Johns Hopkins Paperbacks edition, 2003
9 8 7 6 5 4 3 2 1

The Johns Hopkins University Press
2715 North Charles Street
Baltimore, Maryland 21218-4363
www.press.jhu.edu

LIBRARY OF CONGRESS CATALOGING-IN-PUBLICATION DATA

Ruch, Richard S.
    Higher ed, inc. : the rise of the for-profit university / Richard S. Ruch.
    p.   cm.
  Includes bibliographical references (p.   ) and index.
    ISBN 0-8018-6678-2
    1. Universities and colleges—United States—Finance. 2. Proprietary
  schools—United States—Finance. 3. Vocational education—United States.
  I. Title.
  LB2342 .R72 2001
  378.73—dc21
  00-011514

  ISBN 0-8018-7447-5 (pbk.)

  A catalog record for this book is available from the British Library.

GEORGE KELLER, CONSULTING EDITOR

For my sons, Nathan and Jordan

Contents

Foreword

One of the startling developments in American higher education during the past two decades has been the birth and growth of dozens of new and formidable moneymaking colleges and universities. More than 40 corporations whose securities are traded on the national stock market own and run these institutions. Traditional professors, non-profit campus executives, and many graduates of the nation's 3,400 traditional, accredited colleges and universities—which are charitable, nontaxable, non-profit enterprises worthy of philanthropic gifts, grants, and portions of one's estate—often see this development as a crass intrusion, a sudden sprouting of coarse dandelions on the manicured lawns of higher learning. It seems akin to the Red Cross's or the Sierra Club's abruptly becoming profit-making growth companies, charging big fees for services rendered.

There is also a mounting fascination with these new for-profit colleges and universities. How is it that they can make profits for their owners and shareholders when numerous non-profit colleges run in the red and nearly all have difficulty balancing their budgets? What is it about the historic, lovely, leafy non-profit campuses that makes them so costly and leaves them continually strapped for money? How does the quality of education at these for-profit institutions compare with that of the Ivy League universities, state colleges, and traditional liberal arts colleges? Who on earth are the faculty members at these aggressive corporate universities, and what are the teachers' workloads, salaries, and freedoms? What kinds of students enroll at for-profit colleges instead of cheaper state universities?

Actually, the earliest universities of late medieval times were profit-making corporate associations, and the black gowns that professors still wear at graduations and special events have deep pockets into which students in the thirteenth and fourteenth centuries deposited their fees. Currently, there are more profit-making, proprietary, postsecondary schools and colleges in the United States than there are non-profit institutions. What is novel about the newer for-profit colleges and universities is the joining of the vocational instruction of proprietary schools that teach, say, secretarial science or paralegal studies with solid academic programs that offer traditional baccalaureate, professional, and graduate degrees.

The emergence of serious for-profit institutions of higher education has been prompted by four recent changes. One is the evolution of the economy into a more knowledge-based one. More and more kinds of work in contemporary society require advanced training and education, and higher education for workers is one of the major growth industries of our time. A second is the expansion of adult education. Colleges used to be mainly for young people, 17 to 24 years of age. Today, half of all enrollees in U.S. higher education are over 25 years of age, and among for-profit colleges the percentage is much higher. Third, new electronic technology enables teaching institutions to deliver courses in different ways and at a greater variety of times and places. And fourth, an awakening attention to the management of colleges and universities, which are plagued by costs that are rising one-third faster than the consumer price index, has caused educators to reexamine their modes of operation and the extraordinary, costly array of student services and entertainments they provide.

What Richard Ruch does for the first time in this eye-opening book is take us inside the new for-profit universities. He shows us who teaches there, who enrolls and why, how the for-profits are managed and by whom. And he explains in detail how they make profits instead of requiring lots of red ink. More fundamentally, he analyzes their different structures, services, and outlook on higher learning and training, something that may spark repugnance in some and cause wonder in others. That the for-profits do not offer tenure to their professors alone is enough to raise the hackles of many faculty observers.

Richard Ruch is admirably equipped to reveal the machinery and practices of the booming field of for-profit higher education. He has been a scholarly faculty member and dean at traditional universities and chief academic officer at a campus of one of the for-profit corporations. He knows both worlds intimately. I think you will find this book as enjoyable as it is illuminating because he writes exceedingly well. Like some highly sensate literary scholar, Ruch conveys superbly how it feels to be inside this new kind of institution on the American landscape. He is also candid about the less attractive aspects of the prosperous for-profit colleges and what those who enter them may give up as well as gain.

American higher education has endured and benefited from several fresh additions: the creation of public land-grant colleges to emphasize preparation for work and to open opportunities for the daughters and sons of the working class; the introduction of evening classes and adult education; the construction of a new layer of nearly 1,000 open-admissions, two-year colleges; the spread of primarily research-oriented rather than teaching universities; the racial integration of all colleges; and the use of distance and distributed higher learning and electronic collaborations among campuses. Like these additions, the major for-profit colleges and universities offer a new approach to higher education, an approach that seems sure to influence the more venerable non-profit institutions in the years ahead.

In sum, this book is a marvelous description of a popular, innovative new force for advanced education in the United States. Whom it educates and how it educates should be of keen interest to everyone who cares about the intellectual quality of America's human resources.

GEORGE KELLER

Acknowledgments

To my colleagues at DeVry and other for-profit universities I express gratitude for your opening yourselves and your institutions to me, particularly Michael Markovitz and Jim Otten at Argosy Education Group; Jorge de Alva at Apollo Group; Marla Boulder and Harry Wilkins at Strayer Education; and Stacy Sauchek at Education Management Corporation. At DeVry, I am especially thankful to the following individuals for their encouragement and support: Dennis Keller, Jackie Maresch, Patrick Mayers, Jane Perlmutter, and Wendolyn Tetlow. I also want to acknowledge Robert Bocchino, president of the DeVry New Jersey campus, who taught me much about the business of for-profit higher education.

I am deeply grateful to George Keller for his encouragement and guidance throughout the writing of this book. George introduced me to Jacqueline Wehmueller, editor-in-chief at the Johns Hopkins University Press and editor of this book. To David Bisseeuw and Harold Howard, thank you for your friendship and personal support during this work. Finally, to Renée House, whose brilliance illumines my days, thank you for the gift of believing.

Higher Ed, Inc.

1

Confessions of a For-Profit Dean

I must confess that until a few years ago I thought that all proprietary institutions were the scum of the academic earth. I could not see how the profit motive could properly coexist with an educational mission. While I did not know exactly why I believed this, I was certain in my conviction that non-profit status was noble, just as the profession of education is noble, and that to be for-profit meant to be in it for the money, which was corrupting and ignoble. All the while, I was immune to the irony of the long hours I endured in lunches, dinners, and receptions cultivating potential donors because they had money and my institution needed it. While whole months of my administrative life were spent in meetings about budgets, downsizing, cutting back, and even laying off, I let myself believe that what we were doing was about education and not about money. When my institution created budget forecasts that included provision for excess revenue over expenditures, I did not recognize it as the profit motive. Likewise, I bought into the mythology of the pecking order. I studied and worked in eight different universities that were, for the most part, good ones but not great ones. Except for two semesters at Michigan and one summer at Harvard, I lived in the middle tier of the pecking order. From that vantage point, the proprietary schools were an easy target, serving to locate my institutions in the middle, or perhaps upper middle when compared with the bottom of the barrel.

Having now lived in and studied the view from the other side, I see that I was wrong in my unexamined beliefs about the for-profits, naïve about what it means to be in it for the money, and misinformed about the nature of the profit motive in higher education. With this book I reexamine this sector of American higher education, shattering some of the myths and clarifying the realities of the for-profit sector of the higher-education industry, from its early roots in the evening schools of colonial America to the rapid growth in the 1990s of the large, publicly held, corporate-run universities. What I have learned, and what I hope to substantiate here, is that many of the for-profit providers are actually doing a creditable and even laudable job of addressing educational needs that are in high demand. That is not to say that these organizations are without faults or that there are not some for-profit educational institutions that are substandard in quality and geared more to making profits than to providing education. Just as there is a wide range of quality among traditional, non-profit colleges and universities, there is a range of quality in the for-profit sector. Just as there has been fraud and abuse of public funds in the non-profit sector, there has been fraud and misuse of financial-aid funds in the for-profits. This book focuses on the largest for-profit institutions, which tend to be located at the upper end of the range in institutional quality. If it is true that the American university system is the envy of the world, part of the credit rightly goes to the unrelenting influence of the for-profit sector, which has stood for the application of education in direct response to social and economic needs and the right to turn a profit on a product or service well delivered and which has continued to force change in a system that has stubbornly resisted it.

The Players

The focus of this book is the reemergence of for-profit higher education in the form of large university systems that are owned and operated by publicly traded for-profit corporations. This is not a book about proprietary schools, the small, family-owned businesses run by one or more proprietors who take the profits earned in the business as personal income. Thousands of these schools exist in America and in other countries to meet the demand for training in several trades and regulated industries, such as cosmetology, automotive mechanics, and tourism. Nor is this a book about the hundreds of diploma mills, fake schools that basically sell degrees in any field to customers who cough up $3,000 to $5,000.[1] Neither is this a book about online universities. Although all of the institutions profiled in this book use online instruction to supplement in-class seat time, online education represents a small portion of their business. Finally, this is not a book about what are called "corporate universities," such as Sun Microsystems University, Motorola University, and the University of Toyota. The subject of this book is for-profit colleges and universities that are regionally accredited, degree-granting institutions of higher education that offer programs at the associate, baccalaureate, master's, and doctoral levels. (Five of the major companies in this category are profiled in chapter 2.) Instead of donors they have investors. Instead of endowment they have private investment capital. Instead of being tax-exempt they are tax-paying. As the chapters that follow make clear, these core distinctions set these institutions apart, and that has made all the difference.

Some of the more successful for-profit education providers are relatively new organizations, such as Quest Education, founded in 1988 in Roswell, Georgia, an aggressive acquirer of non-profit colleges (with more than 30 campuses by the year 2000), some of which were facing bankruptcy. Others have been around for many years, such as Strayer University, founded in 1892 in Washington, D.C., and the DeVry Institutes of Technology, founded in 1931 in Chicago. Although the for-profit model in higher education is not new, the creation during the 1990s of publicly traded holding companies that own and run universities is the newest development in a tradition of genteel businesses that existed even before the founding of the first American colleges. Indeed, many of the for-profit providers had humble and quiet births, including the boisterous University of Phoenix, which actually grew out of the humanities department at San Francisco State University in the early 1970s.[2] Similarly, some of today's respectable non-profit colleges and universities actually began as proprietary schools, such as Rider University, which was founded in 1865 in Trenton, New Jersey, as one of the campuses of the Bryant and Stratton chain of business schools, some of which survive to this day.

Institutional Growth and Academic Respectability

The newsworthy story in the for-profit sector during the past decade has been growth and increasing respectability. Since 1990 the number of for-profit, degree-granting college and university campuses in the United States has quietly increased by 112 percent, from approximately 350 to 750 campuses.[3] During the same period at least 200 non-profit colleges closed their doors. The National Center for Higher Education Statistics reported that there were 669 for-profit, degree-granting institutions in the United States in 1996. The Integrated Postsecondary Education Data System indicates that in 1996 about 15 percent of all two- and four-year institutions in the United States were for-profit. It estimated that enrollment in these for-profit colleges and universities was 304,465 in 1996, or 2.1 percent of the total U.S. enrollment of 14,367,530. The number of full-time faculty employed by for-profit, degree-granting institutions in 1996 was estimated to be approximately 26,000, or about 5 percent of the total U.S. full-time faculty of 528,000. For-profit colleges and universities constitute the only sector of the higher-education industry that is growing.* My own prediction, based on a year-long study of the industry, is that the for-profits will continue to grow in number and market share throughout the next decade, whereas growth in the non-profits will continue to decline somewhat.

The increasing respectability of the for-profit institutions and their growing visibility within the higher-education community is evidenced by their meeting and maintaining the standards for accreditation by the regional associations and by other professional accrediting bodies. Argosy Education Group, for example, which offers doctoral programs

---

*The IPEDS data on the number of for-profit institutions is very likely an underestimate. Since the database depends on information volunteered by institutions, and since for many years the Department of Education did not report data on for-profit colleges and universities, a number of for-profit providers probably remain unaccounted for.

through the ten-campus system of the American School of Professional Psychology, is regionally accredited by the North Central Association and has also been successful in gaining accreditation at the doctoral level by the American Psychological Association. Similarly, DeVry's campuses hold both regional accreditation and program accreditation in electronics-engineering technology by the Technology Accreditation Commission of the Accreditation Board for Engineering and Technology. The University of Phoenix is accredited by the North Central Association, and its nursing program is accredited at the baccalaureate and master's levels by the National League for Nursing Accreditation Commission.

The for-profits tend to regard accreditation as a business objective, determining what it will take to meet or exceed the thresholds and then simply allocating the financial and human resources required to meet them. Using this straightforward strategy, they have won the approval of, and often impressed, regional accrediting bodies and their campus-visit teams by meeting and sometimes exceeding the published standards for accreditation. In the past, for-profit institutions struggled to meet the accreditation standards, and even when they did, the accrediting bodies were sometimes reluctant to grant accreditation to these institutions because of their "proprietary" status (see chapter 6). In today's outcomes-assessment environment, to deny accreditation to a for-profit college or university when it meets or exceeds the published standards would probably bring charges of restraint of free trade.

The other aspect of the new respectability of the for-profit providers has to do with the perceived shift in public attitudes toward corporate America and the free-market economy in general. During the final decade of the twentieth century the profit motive seems to have lost some of its association with evil intent. The for-profit universities caught the wave of renewed belief in, and fascination with, corporate enterprise and the performance of the stock market in particular. Even small investors who had no money in the stock market other than perhaps an IRA or part of a 401k or a retirement annuity, such as TIAA-CREF, have done very well during the past ten years. At the same time that the profit motive was enjoying a renaissance of sorts, non-profit organizations were facing greater public scrutiny, in part because of scandals over alleged excessive lobbying, fraud, and mismanagement at such institutions as United Way of America, Toys for Tots, the NAACP, and Stanford University.

"These are difficult days for America's non-profits," writes Charles Kolb, general counsel for United Way and former official at the U.S. Department of Education (DOE). Kolb sees the Stanford scandal—which broke in 1991, when the university was accused of excessive indirect cost rates and misuse of federal research dollars—as "the beginning episode that brought the 'age of accountability' to American postsecondary education in particular and to the non-profit sector more generally."[4] Stanford was ultimately cleared of any criminal charges involving fraud, but the issue of mismanagement had become a major part of the national higher-education agenda. By the mid-1990s nonprofit universities were facing what Kolb describes as the third wave of accountability. Higher education was relatively untouched by the first wave, which hit American corporations in the 1980s, as global competitiveness, stockholder demands, and emerging technologies caused massive layoffs and restructuring. The second wave, directed at big government during the Reagan and Bush administrations, targeted government spending and the national deficit. But again, in Kolb's assessment, this second wave of accountability did not significantly impact higher education. The third wave, however, starting with the Stanford case, led to new demands for accountability, the new emphasis on outcomes assessment in the regional accreditation standards, and the language of value added throughout the higher-education industry. At the heart of the accountability issue, says Kolb, is the question of how to measure the value added of a college education. "The sad fact," he laments, "is we don't yet know the answer."[5]

Yet the for-profit colleges and universities do have an answer. For them, the value added of a college education is what Dennis Keller, chairman of DeVry, calls "career launching." The usual metric for assessing value added is the significantly greater earning power of a college graduate compared with that of a non-college graduate (currently about twice as much). The earning-power argument is a difficult pill to swallow for many traditional educators, for it reduces the sacred ideals of higher education, in particular the *artes liberales* ideal, to an economic-return equation. However, this loss of ideals—or to put it more gently, this narrowing of ideals—is what has happened in American higher education, where today even elite institutions often use the earn-ing power of graduates to justify the price of tuition.[6]

The issue of measuring the payoff of a college degree by the earning power of graduates is addressed more fully in chapter 6. The point here is that the for-profit providers are abler than most non-profits to deliver a direct response to the demand for value-added measurement. Indeed, their corporate environment already requires such measure-ment as a routine part of business operations.

The Question of Educational Quality

One of the most enduring myths about for-profit educational institu-tions is that they generally offer a poor-quality education to students. "Many of our colleagues in the traditional academy still believe we are all snake oil sales people," says Jack Sites, CEO and provost of Argosy Education's American Schools of Professional Psychology and a former official with the Southern Association of Colleges and Schools. He adds: "They continue to hang on to the self-serving myth that we are selling products of sub-par quality for too much money to students who could not get in anywhere else."[7]

In a somewhat kinder judgment, it is often assumed that, at best, what the for-profits provide to students is employability, and not neces-sarily education.[8] Of course, they do offer employability, and not only is that one of their strengths but it is what a large segment of higher education's consumers expect from a college education. The for-profit providers have aligned themselves with the public's expectation that a good college education should result in employability. Employability, however, is not all they provide, for real teaching and learning also occur in these institutions. In my experience, when good teachers work with motivated students, real learning often results. All of the for-profit providers profiled in this book have both numerous good teachers and a large proportion of highly motivated students.

Some educators who assume that for-profit schools offer a poor-qual-ity education have asserted that the for-profit providers are subject to less regulation and oversight than are the non-profit institutions.[9] In fact, as publicly held companies, they have oversight and regulatory requirements that go beyond those faced by non-profit institutions, such as quarterly reports to the Securities and Exchange Commission.

Others suggest, incorrectly, that for-profit providers are notorious for allegations of fraud and conspiracy. My own review of the literature suggests that there are at least as many actual instances of fraud and mismanagement in the non-profit sector, perhaps more. And Jack Sites observes, "If the journalistic community in America did not hold traditional universities in such high regard, they would find an incredible story in the revelation that higher education is absolutely rife with corruption, fraud, and mismanagement."[10] There is also a lingering belief, deep within the consciousness of the traditional academy, that profits and the market generally are fundamentally antithetical to serving the needs of society and of students.

It is not clear, at least to me, when or how it became a virtue for a university to be organized on a non-profit basis instead of a for-profit one. We know that our earliest universities were strongly and directly tied to the churches in terms of both finances and mission. Perhaps the virtuousness of non-profit status for the university grew out of this early association with churches. Regardless, my own sense is that for-profit or non-profit status is not in and of itself a determinant of institutional quality. A similar point was recently made in a study of the health-care industry, which is undergoing a transformation in teaching hospitals from non-profit to for-profit status.[11] Initially, some medical-school officials found this trend alarming and were concerned that the for-profit companies would cut back and eliminate unprofitable services that were nonetheless important to the hospital's mission. Conducted by two researchers at the Harvard Medical School, the study examined the impact on the teaching mission of hospitals that were sold to for-profit corporations. No negative impacts were found on teaching, medical education, research, or indigent care. In effect, the changeover to for-profit status did not impact the quality of education or the social good one way or the other.

It must also be said that the academy and society in general have for centuries debated the question of what constitutes a proper, quality education. The debate that began in ancient Greek and Roman philosophy about whether the focus of education should be on training the intellect or cultivating noble virtues has not been resolved.[12] No clear, uniform understanding has emerged about what constitutes a proper university education. Instead, there are several different models and philosophies of higher education, just as there is considerable mission diversity among universities. The for-profit institutions are simply part of higher education's philosophical diversity and multiple missions.

The popular assertion that the American system of higher education is the envy of the world, a claim that is routinely heard at the plenary sessions of academic conventions ranging from the Modern Language Association to the American Assembly of Collegiate Schools of Business, is sometimes delivered as a kind of reminder that things could be worse. The basis for the claim that the American system is the best in the world is not always apparent, but clearly the United States spends more on education than any other nation—about $750 billion, more than twice as much as on defense, with about $340 billion going to higher education—and American universities continue to attract large numbers of foreign students, especially at the graduate level.

Still, many higher-education insiders continue to sound eschatological alarms, ranging from such thoughtful books as Jaroslav Pelikan's *Idea of the University,* Bill Readings's *University in Ruins,* and Bruce Wilshire's *Moral Collapse of the University* to books about corruption within the academy and some that point to the "corporatization" of the university as the root problem, such as Nelson and Watt's witty and self-conscious *Academic Keywords.* [13] These books raise many issues about the present state of higher education in America and its future. None of them and few presenters of plenary speeches at academic conventions are warm to the idea of applying the corporate model to higher education. Some are quick to cite the emergence and growth of such for-profit providers as the University of Phoenix, which is seen as an extreme application of the corporate model where it probably does not belong, as a clear sign of end times. Given the concern about the rapid growth of the for-profit purveyors and the constant claims that higher education is in crisis, collapsing, and headed for ruin, it is not clear just what the rest of the world is envying.

The overlooked and somewhat hidden aspect of the unfolding story of higher education in America is the for-profit sector, which has been present as a mostly silent but nonetheless influential partner in the founding, development, and evolution of the American system of higher education right from the beginning. The rich and deep history of proprietary education in America (see chapter 3) attests to the fact that these institutions developed and matured alongside of, and not apart from, traditional colleges and universities. A true understanding of both the tradition and the future of higher education in this country must account for them.

For-Profit and Non-Profit Distinctions

What is clear is that for-profit and non-profit universities tend to operate under different hierarchies of institutional and organizational values. These different hierarchies of values are revealed in a number of distinctions that can be made between non-profit and for-profit institutions. Table 1.1 shows ten such distinctions that, taken individually, provide a breakdown of salient points of difference and, taken collectively, provide an overall picture of how these types of institutions differ. Each set of distinctions is briefly described below and discussed further in subsequent chapters.

TAX-EXEMPT / TAX-PAYING

One of the obvious areas of difference is taxation. Milton Friedman, the Nobel laureate economist, has suggested that the terms *for-profit* and *non-profit* should be dropped altogether from the higher-education lexicon in favor of the more descriptive *tax paying* and *tax-exempt*.[14] Indeed, the essential financing distinction between non-profit and for-

Table 1.1 Non-Profit and For-Profit Distinctions in Higher Education

Non-Profit	For-Profit
Tax-exempt	Tax-paying
Donors	Investors
Endowment	Private investment capital
Stakeholders	Stockholders
Shared governance	Traditional management
Prestige motive	Profit motive
Cultivation of knowledge	Application of learning
Discipline-driven	Market-driven
Quality of inputs	Quality of outcomes
Faculty power	Customer power

profit universities is not a matter of profitability or the profit motive but one of taxation, as both a source of revenue and a form of expenditure (see chapter 4). In essence, non-profit institutions are, by definition, exempt from paying taxes. In fact, non-profit colleges and universities, including all public and most private institutions, receive tax subsidies to support their operations. Public colleges and universities receive an average of 50 percent of their revenues in the form of tax subsidies from federal, state, and local governments, while private non-profit colleges and universities receive about 17 percent.[15] The for-profits, of course, receive no tax subsidies. Instead, they have a substantial tax burden, with most education companies setting aside about 40 percent of earnings before taxes for paying taxes. These differences in the tax status of the institutions represent fundamental differences in the way they are organized as corporate entities. For example, the non-profits are oriented toward maximizing the tax subsidies they receive, whereas the for-profits are oriented toward minimizing the tax they must pay on profits.

DONORS / INVESTORS

Non-profit institutions have donors, and the corollary on the for-profit side is investors. Donated income is a key source of operating revenue and financial security for non-profit institutions, and the same is true for the for-profit institutions, for which "donations" come in the form of stock purchases. Non-profits spend considerable energy on the cultivation of potential donors, while for-profits cultivate the investment community. In some respects this cultivation work is similar, particularly because it involves promoting the institution to audiences that have financial resources to donate or invest.

Yet there are differences as well. For one, the cultivation of donors on the non-profit side often involves many members of the institution. Not only the chief development officer and the president but also academic deans, members of the faculty, and even students perform fund-raising work. On the for-profit side, only senior management, supported by one or two professional staff members, cultivates investors. As an academic dean at DeVry, I have never been involved in fund-raising of any kind, but as an academic dean in non-profit universities I spent as much as a third of my time on fund-raising. A second difference is that while both donors and investors have an interest in how their financial support is used, investors also expect a financial return. Investors bring an added dimension of accountability for operating the institution in ways that ensure profitability and future earnings.

ENDOWMENT / PRIVATE INVESTMENT CAPITAL

The third distinction follows from the second. Donated income is accumulated in the form of endowment in the non-profits, while stock purchases in the for-profits take the form of private investment capital. Endowment and private investment capital function similarly in each sector, providing the financial foundation for long-term solvency and investment income that can also be used to support current operations. Non-profit universities, like other individual and corporate investors, invest all or part of their endowment funds in the stock and bond markets. When these investments earn dividends, the non-profit sector returns a portion to the endowment. When the for-profits earn dividends on their private investment capital, they return a portion to the stockholder. Both endowment and private investment capital, then, are invested for the purpose of realizing growth, and a portion of that growth is returned to either the donated fund or the investor.

Attracting money, whether in the form of donors or investors, requires the ability to inspire confidence. When a traditional university is able to build a substantial endowment fund, it not only ensures the institution's future but also economically affirms the institution's reason for being. When alumni, corporations, private foundations, state governments, and wealthy individuals donate money to a university, the institution is affirmed in powerful and tangible ways. In essence donors are saying, "We believe in you." The same is true in the for-profit sector when investors "donate" their money to an educational company through the purchase of its stock. When private citizens and corporate investors buy ownership in a university through stock purchases, the institution's financial future is secured and its reason for being is affirmed. Both the for-profits and the non-profits depend on other people's money for their solvency and long-term survival. The for-profit model is stockholder-driven, while the non-profit model is stakeholder-driven.

STAKEHOLDERS / STOCKHOLDERS

The stockholder-driven model appears on the surface to be vastly simpler than the stakeholder-driven model. Stockholders all want the same thing, namely, a return on their investment. To ensure a steady influx of private investment capital, the for-profits must demonstrate an ability to generate a return to stockholders in the form of equity. The simple barometer of how well a publicly traded company performs is, of course, the changing value of its stock. When the stock price goes up, investors make money, and when the stock price goes down, they lose money. The actual gain or loss does not occur, of course, unless the stock is actually sold off. However, the factors that can influence changes in the value of stock are often complex and are influenced by variables outside the control of the company, such as global economic trends and demographic shifts. Of necessity, this adds a certain amount of unpredictability to the company's performance, which in turn adds risk to stockholders. Even when the financial indicators look good, investors will sometimes bail out. Investors buy stock when they feel confident, and consumer confidence is a complex equation.

One of the interesting features of the stockholder-driven model in higher education is employee ownership. Faculty members, for example, along with the deans, presidents, and even the registrars and admissions representatives, often own stock in for-profit universities. This stock may be accumulated through an employee stock-purchase program or a 401k retirement program, or it may be awarded in the form of stock options. DeVry recently gave all full-time employees stock-option awards based on years of service. Aside from being a nice gesture, it was an astute business decision. When faculty members, for example, also become investors in their university through stock ownership, they soon develop a personal stake not only in academic matters but also in the financial success of the enterprise. When the company that owns the university is profitable, everyone who owns stock shares in the profits.

In contrast, stakeholders—students and their families, faculty members, administrators, trustees, alumni, donors, employers, accreditation bodies, community leaders, government agencies—have varied and sometimes incompatible interests and concerns. Trustees, for example, may argue for a reduction in faculty release time from teaching, while certain program-accrediting bodies encourage more release time for research and scholarly activity. Many college and university presidents, along with many other administrators, spend much of their time responding to these stakeholders. Although for-profit institutions must deal with many of these same stakeholders as well, their first priority is to the stockholders. Built into the stakeholder-driven model, of course, is the idea that many persons should have their say, which requires an enormous amount of time and patience and often stagnates the decision-making process. This emphasis on participation and inclusion of everyone who has a stake in the institution brings up the fifth distinction: shared governance versus traditional management.

SHARED GOVERNANCE / TRADITIONAL MANAGEMENT

The concept of shared governance is deeply ingrained in the culture of the non-profit university. In the British, French, and German universities, for example, the faculty senates are said to wield considerably more power than the rectors.[16] By comparison, American university presidents and provosts appear to have more formal power, although they often feel powerless. "Shared governance is an enlightened concept," says Scott S. Cowen, president of Tulane University, "but in execution it may actually be a deterrent to the future of higher education."[17] Cowen is outspoken about the "new competitive scenario unlike anything we've seen before" in traditional higher education, resulting in part from the rise and success of the new for-profit providers. Consequently, he wants his institution and others to be able to make at least some major decisions quickly and effectively. Standing in the way of quick, effective decision making is the tradition of shared governance. "The real zealots of shared governance lecture that shared governance is an end in itself," he says. "It is not."[18]

Yet shared governance is deeply woven into the fabric of the university, even on the for-profit side, although these corporations have an advantage: the for-profits can and do reappropriate the concept of shared governance, applying it to certain areas and excluding it from others. In my experience, the management strategy of the for-profits is to allow enough shared governance to appease regional accreditation visiting teams and keep the faculty from unionizing. In so doing, the for-profits retain management control of the decision-making process while still making some provision for shared governance. For example, faculty in the for-profits do not have tenure, which changes the balance of power between the faculty member (employee) and the institution (employer). Yet the faculty in the for-profits do enjoy a reasonable measure of academic freedom, and they participate fully in decisions regarding the curriculum. In other areas, however, such as admission requirements, the for-profit faculty do not have much of a voice. (The issues of tenure, academic freedom, and organizational culture in the for-profit institutions are addressed in chapter 5.)

The governance structures and processes of the for-profit university are based on the values of traditional corporate management. Accountability for certain outcomes is fixed with individual managers, who have both the responsibility and the authority to make decisions. In these environments, governance is not "shared" in the way the traditional academy has operationalized the term. The reason for this can be summarized in one word—bosses.

One of the realities of working in for-profit universities is the presence of bosses, and this is especially true of the multicampus organizations controlled by a home office. Everyone on these campuses has at least one boss, often two or three, and there is no mistaking who they are: they conduct and sign your annual performance appraisal, which directly affects your compensation and promotability. In contrast, the collegial model of traditional universities intentionally blurs the distinction between bosses and colleagues. The dean wants to be your colleague, as does the provost and even the president, and while they are also bosses in the technical sense, they are encouraged to embrace this role apologetically. In the for-profits your boss is clearly not your colleague but your superior, and you are his or her employee, subordinate in rank, authority, responsibility, and power. Any modicum of shared governance is inevitably split unequally, and the boss must sanction any pretense of genuine collegiality. In many American corporations today there are some enlightened and progressive leaders and managers, but the for-profit higher-education companies are all managed conservatively according to tried-and-true methods of supervision. (The management culture of the for-profits, with its emphasis on the supervision of work, along with an explanation for why this conservative approach has so far worked fairly successfully, is discussed more fully in chapter 5.)

PRESTIGE MOTIVE / PROFIT MOTIVE

A sixth distinction describes an underlying motive that drives the institution toward the achievement of its goals and mission. The non-profits are driven by what I call the prestige motive, as opposed to the profit motive on the for-profit side. The prestige motive is the desire to move up in the pecking order of perceived ranking among competing institutions. All colleges and universities have a group of other institutions to which they like to compare themselves, whether it's the Ivy League, the second tier, the best buys, or a group of neighboring competitors. Despite questions about the methodologies used in the college rankings published in such popular magazines as *Money* and *U.S. News & World Reports,* these rankings are taken seriously by most institutions listed in them, and those excluded want to get on the lists. As some institutions grow and mature, they often seem to fall into a kind of Harvard-in-the-small mentality, seeking to add more signs of prestige, such as endowed chairs, and even changing their institutional names to reflect greater respectability. Many state colleges have fought to be called universities, and some have also dropped the word *state* from their names, such as Memphis State University, which used to be called Memphis State College and is now called the University of Memphis. The drive for greater prestige sometimes compels institutions to take actions that anger alumni and alienate the local community, such as Trenton State College's decision to change its name to the College of New Jersey, a decision that still irks the city fathers in Trenton as well as the old guard at Princeton University (which was originally founded as the College of New Jersey).

The for-profits, on the other hand, are not particularly interested in prestige; they are driven by the profit motive. (I argue in chapter 4 that the profit motive is actually alive in non-profit colleges and universities, albeit not with the same visibility and force as in the for-profits.) Profitability is imperative in an enterprise structured on the stockholder model, and at the for-profit universities the profit motive translates into a kind of bottom-line discipline that impacts the whole organization. In such an environment, the academic side of the house becomes a tightly managed service operation, for the for-profit providers regard the class-room as the place where revenue is generated and costs are the highest.

In the simplest of terms, the for-profit universities have taken a highly traditional model of education—a teacher in front of a class of students—and run it like a business. Scale economies and operating efficiencies are deployed to the fullest extent, with the result that the familiar inefficiencies of the traditional college in such areas as space utilization, class size, and efficient deployment of faculty, are minimized. (The "luxury of inefficiency" in traditional higher education is discussed in chapter 6.)

The faculty, which in all educational institutions represents the single largest recurring financial expenditure, are fully deployed to teach in the for-profit institutions. At traditional universities, faculty are typically released from a third to a half of their teaching time for other responsibilities, primarily research, administration or governance, and service activities. Such release time may be a necessary investment in a research university, but in the applications-oriented for-profit environment it is considered a nonproductive expense that cannot be leveraged into profitability. The heavier teaching loads (usually four to five classes a week) and almost total lack of release time for research and minimal release time for governance represent significant cost savings in the for-profit institutions.

Yet it is not merely efficiencies and scale economies that result in profitability. My years in the for-profit educational sector have taught me that the two factors above all others that drive profitability are educational quality and customer service. No for-profit college or university can survive without providing both a reasonably high-quality educational experience and a high level of customer service. If someone imagines that these institutions make profits merely because they offer a substandard education on a massive scale, they are largely mistaken. Student consumers, especially the more mature students typical of the for-profit providers, are knowledgeable and demanding customers who are not easily satisfied. They demand a substantive and rigorous educational experience for their tuition dollars, along with a high level of convenience and customer service. And if they do not find it, they will go elsewhere.

Why and how the for-profits are profitable while many traditional non-profit institutions struggle to break even is discussed in detail in chapter 4, where the downsides of the profit motive—greed and the emphasis on sales—are also considered. The point here is that the for-profits replace the prestige motive with the profit motive.

CULTIVATION OF KNOWLEDGE / APPLICATION OF LEARNING

In fundamental ways the major universities are now focused on the generation of knowledge and the advancement of the disciplines through basic and applied research, experimentation, and discovery. The value of such work permeates the whole of such institutions, and some would say it is at the very heart of the idea of the university. Liberal arts colleges represent another valued tradition related to the cultivation of knowledge, in this case for more intrinsic and less extrinsic ends, through the training of the intellect and the development of moral habits and virtues.[19] The generation, dissemination, and advancement of knowledge are core values that are protected by academic freedom and more or less woven into the mission statement of virtually every respectable, traditional academic institution. Even the for-profit providers do not totally ignore these values, for they are more or less built into accreditation and state licensing standards. While DeVry, for example, offers no degrees in the liberal arts, 50 percent of the coursework in the baccalaureate programs at the New Jersey campus is in the liberal arts and sciences, as required by the state of New Jersey. All of higher education is deeply influenced by the values associated with what I call here the cultivation of knowledge. Indeed, a recent study of faculty-incentive systems published by the National Center for Postsecondary Education Improvement concluded that "the research model has come to pervade all types of institutions of higher education."[20]

Yet there is another view of what it means to be in the knowledge business. This view acknowledges the value of generating new knowledge but also recognizes another important priority, the application of knowledge that already exists to solve practical problems. As I illustrate in chapter 3, this focus on the application of knowledge, along with the development of skills, to solve problems has been the primary focus of the for-profit sector of higher education since its beginnings in colonial America. This focus requires being closely attuned to the current needs of the marketplace, especially in areas where there is a strong, unmet demand for specialized education and training.

DISCIPLINE-DRIVEN / MARKET-DRIVEN

Market responsiveness is the key to the success of the for-profit players. The phenomenal growth of the University of Phoenix during the last ten years, for example, is essentially the result of timing and successful market positioning. Phoenix jumped out ahead of all competitors by being at the right place at the right time with the right products and services. As the adult population grew to represent 50 percent of all college students, Phoenix was there with what many of them were looking for, described by Jorge de Alva, Phoenix's president, as the demand for "a professional, businesslike relationship with their campus that is characterized by convenience, cost- and time-effective services and education, predictable and consistent quality, seriousness of purpose, and high customer service geared to their needs, not those of faculty members, administrators, or staff."[21] Such a description holds true for DeVry, Strayer, Education Management, and Argosy, each of which has identified a unique market niche within the vast marketplace of U.S. higher education's 15 million students.

Market responsiveness requires that an institution adapt to rapid, discontinuous change. Curricula must be updated quickly and continuously, new programs must be developed and launched while the market need is extant, and existing courses and programs that no longer meet current demand must be dropped. Many traditional, non-profit colleges and universities are unresponsive or slow to respond in these ways because they are discipline-driven, not market-driven. While the for-profits listen to the marketplace, the non-profits listen mainly to the disciplines.

Academic disciplines are controlled by the faculty and tend to change slowly, deliberately, and incrementally. The traditional model places a high value on allowing the disciplines and their professors to play the lead role in guiding change in academic programs; as a result, the change process in many of these institutions is evolutionary. Tenured faculty must be deployed even if there is low demand for their disciplines. In addition to the traditional emphasis on inclusiveness, collaboration, and consensus, the discipline-driven institution is less concerned with the marketplace and less able to respond to it quickly.

QUALITY OF OUTCOMES / QUALITY OF INPUTS

In allocating resources and assessing educational quality the for-profits tend to place greater emphasis on educational outputs—student satisfaction, retention rates, completion rates, and placement rates—while the non-profits have traditionally placed a higher value on inputs—admissions selectivity, faculty credentials, and an array of extracurricular programs and activities. Student placement, for example, is carefully measured in the for-profit environment, where it is generally supported by a relatively large investment in human, physical, and financial resources. At my own DeVry campus, for example, with an enrollment of 3,500 students, the placement office is staffed by 13 full-time employees, 10 of whom are professional placement advisers. This represents a much larger placement operation than found at most non-profit institutions. As a consequence, the placement rate at DeVry has hovered around 95 percent for more than 10 years running, a rate considerably higher than at most traditional undergraduate colleges and universities. Clearly, student placement is a high core value at DeVry, and a key outcomes metric in assessing institutional quality.

In contrast, a number of traditional non-profit institutions do not measure and report student-placement rates. Instead, they tend to place a higher value on such input measures as student selectivity and entering SAT and ACT scores, which are carefully measured and reported as an indication of institutional quality and ranking in the pecking order.

FACULTY POWER / CUSTOMER POWER

The 10th and final distinction concerns the locus of power within the institution. In most, perhaps all, of the non-profits the faculty are the focus of power within the governance structure. Longstanding tradition, the dominance of the disciplines, the tenure system, the principle of academic freedom, shared governance, and the presence of collective bargaining on many campuses have all contributed to strengthening and protecting the power of the faculty. In the for-profit environment the role of the faculty is more limited, and they generally do not have as much institutional power. The strong customer orientation on the campuses of Phoenix, DeVry, Education Management, Argosy, and Strayer shifts the center of gravity. At these institutions, the students and the managers (or bosses) are the focus of power. (This shift and its implications on the life of the institution is analyzed further in chapter 5.)

Crossing Over to the For-Profit Side

Those of us who have left traditional universities and crossed over to for-profit institutions feel a certain kinship. What many of us have discovered is that the for-profit way of doing education is not so much better or worse than the non-profit way; it is just a different approach. Many who have crossed over find that there is a certain refreshing honesty associated with being openly for-profit, a welcoming lack of pretense in the economic exchange between students and their institutions. Administrators who have worked in both camps (and even some of the faculty) find that not having to deal with the tenure system is a relief.

There have been many times when I truly enjoyed the administrative freedom of actually making decisions and implementing them. It has been satisfying, for example, to see a new degree program for which there is strong market demand go from idea to implementation within twelve months. I have felt effective and responsible to my students in being able to handle a few cases involving faculty members who were, simply put, terrible classroom teachers. One, for example, was a professor who was abusing his female students through inappropriate language, extreme suggestiveness, and outright propositioning. I witnessed this behavior firsthand, as did others on the faculty. It was gratifying for me to be able to get this person out of the classroom immediately. That would have never happened in a traditional academic environment, where the concern for due process would have prevented me from taking immediate action.

And yet, I must confess that for traditional academic types like me there is also a certain sense of loss in moving into the for-profit environment. I was weaned on the ideals of collegiality and shared governance, and I regard these ideals as noble, enlightened, and worth striving for. At DeVry, in my work with the academic deans and the faculty

I often have found myself pulled between my natural instincts for collegial decision making and my company's impatience with the inefficiency that results from inclusiveness and debate. In addition, on some occasions during my years at DeVry I have felt that the faculty were not treated with the kind of respect and professionalism they deserved. For example, my campus often plans faculty colloquia during semester breaks on topics generated by the faculty themselves. Even though 90 percent of the faculty participate in these events, the upper managers have urged me to take attendance, make of list of those who do not attend, and perhaps even dock their paychecks accordingly. I resist this practice because I think it is insulting to the faculty, but I feel an acute sense of loss in the fact that my bosses asked me to do it. I want us instead to honor the principle of attraction, making these colloquia so stimulating and relevant that nearly 100 percent of the faculty will make it a point to be there. If only 90 percent show up (which still seems quite remarkable to me), it simply means we need to do a better job of making these events more attractive.

In my twenty years as an administrator in a private, urban university, a state land-grant university, a liberal arts college, and now a for-profit provider, I have worked during periods of growth and expansion and periods of decline and cutting back. Growth is definitely more satisfying. Building new campuses, hiring new faculty, and generally having plenty of cash to spend on technology, faculty travel, and new program development all make for a stimulating experience. If, like me, you like the idea of working in an institution that is somewhat of a renegade, needing to prove its worthiness to the skeptics but also possessing the financial resources to do so, then the for-profit environment can be an exciting place to be.

Still, there is this sense of loss, call it sadness, a gentle melancholy known in Buddhism as "the death of dreams." In an engaging article in the *New Yorker* entitled "Drive-Thru U," James Traub writes that "the traditional American university occupies a space that is both bounded and pastoral—a space that speaks of monastic origins and a commitment to unworldliness."[22] For-profits are by design decidedly worldly. Traub puts it this way: "The institution that sees itself as the steward of intellectual culture is becoming increasingly marginal; the others are racing to accommodate the new student."

Those time-honored, laudable ideals—shared governance, the life of the mind, learning for its own sake—sometimes haunt me in my dreams like a secret lover. Something ancient in my heart of hearts resists the notion that efficiency and practicality should define the greatest good. There are real losses in this shift in values, and I suspect that all of us in academia, regardless of our institutional affiliation, have felt them to some degree.

Perhaps that is why I so enjoyed being a member of the mural committee, a group of ten students and faculty who designed and painted a mural over the course of two semesters on a 50-foot wall in the student commons area of my DeVry campus. The painting of the mural was a case study in how individual artistic expression and shared, community vision can work in harmony. We worked collaboratively on our 50-foot wall, sometimes dealing with disagreement but managing somehow to respect one another's individual artistic sensibilities while also adapting our personal styles to create one whole work. There were days when I felt that this was the most important and fulfilling work I did.

2
The Players

The primary subject of this book, as noted in the previous chapter, is not proprietary schools as they have been known and understood but rather a newer model of educational institution: accredited, degree-granting colleges and universities owned and operated by publicly held, for-profit corporations. From the standpoint of their structure and operations, these institutions may have more in common with multi-campus, public, non-profit universities than they do with traditional proprietary schools. They are owned by, and accountable to, not a proprietor but the public in the form of thousands of stockholders. Their budgets are determined once a year through negotiations with their holding companies, not unlike the negotiations between public universities and state legislative bodies. Their success is ultimately determined by how well they serve the needs of students and employers in their regions.

Of course, there are also significant differences between these institutions and public universities. Interestingly, however, these differences do not stem primarily from the distinction between their for-profit and non-profit statuses, which, as I argue in chapter 4, is basically a distinction grounded in the language of accounting and the law and practices of taxation. The real differences appear to have more to do with institutional missions and organizational culture. Instead of the traditional "teaching, research, and service" mission of the public (and private, non-profit, for that matter) universities, the for-profit providers have highly focused missions, targeted to specific market segments, particular industries, and limited to specific fields of study. Unlike most public universities, they are very clear about what they will not do.

Deciding what will not be part of the institutional mission, and therefore not part of the budget, curriculum, and work of the faculty, has been one of the intractable problems facing many non-profit colleges and universities, especially the many small or medium-sized institutions with limited resources. At one regional university where I worked as an academic dean the president's council struggled for years with the question how to focus the mission of the institution. In essence, this struggle boiled down to deciding what the mission statement should not include, which meant that something had to go. The deeper problem was that this institution had struggled for decades to be recognized as a "comprehensive university," which seemed to imply that it must offer majors and degree programs in just about everything. The history department, for example, had five full-time faculty members and about the same number of history majors. Meanwhile, programs with high student demand, such as business administration and psychology, were starved for resources. The desire to be "comprehensive" also translated into increasing demands on the faculty to publish in peer-reviewed journals in order to get tenure. Release time for scholarly work escalated, standard teaching loads were reduced from twelve to nine hours, and increasing numbers of adjunct faculty were hired to do the teaching. Despite all the proper rhetoric about how scholarship is supposed to inform good teaching, the reality at this institution was that the value system was changed and financial and human resources were shifted away from teaching.

Fundamental Questions about For-Profit Educational Institutions

In the for-profit institutional environment, research and scholarly productivity are excluded or at least significantly downplayed in institutional mission statements. Basic research and scholarship is one category of things that these institutions have decided they will not do. This exclusion raises questions about how they, as universities, contribute to the advancement of knowledge. Their lack of a tenure system and reliance on part-time, practitioner faculty brings into question their commitment to academic freedom and their ability to maintain an intellectual center. Because their curricula are limited to fields for which there is high, unmet, occupational demand, such as telecommunications and information technology, they do not offer majors or degree programs in the many fields with low occupational demand, such as physics, history, English literature, or American studies. They are highly customer oriented, which leads to the question whether they are able to sustain reasonable academic rigor and resist giving away good grades for the sake of happy customers. They tend to be less selective in admissions, providing greater access to working adults, the large population of students who are below average academically, and students who are economically, socially, and politically marginalized. These issues beg the general question whether these institutions represent yet a further watering down of the term *university*, especially because they appear to be without apology in the business of job training. Larger questions also arise about whether these institutions are truly serving society or merely turning a profit by providing a service for a fee.

These are all fundamental questions that are addressed throughout this book. The answers have implications for all of higher education. Research universities, liberal arts colleges, regional state colleges and universities, the less well endowed private institutions, and two-year institutions are all becoming more customer oriented and market sensitive. Many institutions are using more adjunct faculty, and many that do not appear to meet the classic definition have changed their names to "university." These kinds of changes have been on the radar screens of colleges and universities for many years. What has been alarming to many educators in non-profit institutions is that the for-profit providers have tended to move more quickly and effectively to embrace these changes. As noted in chapter 1, the for-profit sector is the only segment of the higher-education industry that is growing in terms of enrollment, numbers of institutions, and market share. These institutions have apparently hit a highly responsive chord with an increasing number of students, employers, private investors, and even a growing number of traditional faculty members, who are crossing over to the for-profit side and giving up tenure for stock options.

Who are these for-profit players, where did they come from, what it is like to live, work, and study in them, and how much of the higher-education market are they likely to capture? To help address these kinds of questions and give clearer definition to this segment of the higher-education industry, I have selected five major providers for closer description. These five are referred to throughout this book and used, along with selected others, as examples to describe institutional development and growth, financing, operating practices, and various aspects of academic culture in for-profit institutions. These five providers are: the Apollo Group, Inc. (University of Phoenix); Argosy Education Group (American Schools of Professional Psychology); DeVry, Inc. (DeVry Institutes of Technology); Education Management Corporation (Art Institutes International); and Strayer Education, Inc. (Strayer University). Table 2.1 provides basic descriptive information on all five.

Together these five represent more than 244 individual campuses (including about 100 "instructional sites" that would not normally be considered campuses) with a combined enrollment of about 190,000 students in 2000. They were selected from among a field of approximately 45 corporations listed on the stock exchange that offer college degrees, and they are representative of the program diversity currently available in the for-profit sector. Each of these five companies is unique in terms of its educational focus, its history, and its academic culture. Each intends to attract particular kinds of students who are generally viewed as being underserved by traditional institutions.

Let us begin by identifying the kinds of students these institutions serve and then proceed with a more up-close and personal tour of each of the five corporations.

Table 2.1 Profiles of Five For-Profit Players

Name	Founded, IPO	Core Institutions	Campuses	Enrollment	Programs	Accreditation
Apollo Group, Inc. Phoenix, Ariz. (NASDAQ: APOL)	1976, 1994	University of Phoenix Institute for Professional Development Western International University College for Financial Planning	137 in United States and Puerto Rico	100,000	Diploma through master's	North Central plus other professional
Argosy Education Group Chicago, Ill. (NASDAQ: ARGY)	1975, 1999	American Schools of Professional Psychology University of Sarasota John Marshall Law School Prime-Tech Institute Ventura Group	17 in 7 states	5,000	Mainly doctorate and master's; also others	North Central, American Psychological Association
DeVry, Inc. Chicago, Ill. (NYSE: DV)	1931, 1991	DeVry Institutes of Technology Keller Graduate Schools of Management Denver Technical College Becker Conviser CPA Review	19 campuses in 10 states and Canada; 30 Keller sites	50,000	Certificate through master's	North Central, Accreditation Board for Engineering Technology
Education Management Corporation Pittsburgh, Pa. (NASDAQ: EDMC)	1962, 1996	Art Institutes International New York Restaurant School National Center for Paralegal Training	20 in 17 cities	20,000	Certificate through bachelor's	North Central, New England, Southern Association
Strayer Education, Inc. Washington, D.C. (NASDAQ: STRA)	1982, 1996	Strayer University	12 in 3 states	12,500	Associate through master's	Middle States

The Students of the For-Profit Universities

The students who attend for-profit universities are as diverse a group as those attending most institutions, ranging from unemployed 18-year-olds just out of high school to middle-aged professionals looking for career advancement. One-third of DeVry's 50,000 students, for example, are recent high-school graduates and fit the demographic profile of typical college freshmen, although they tend to be somewhat less well prepared academically. Most of the 20,000 students attending Education Management Corporation's art institutes are in their early twenties, unemployed or employed part time in jobs they want to leave. The typical student enrolled at the University of Phoenix, with an enrollment of 100,000, is 35 years old, employed full time at a professional level, with an annual income of $56,000. At the University of Sarasota, an Argosy Education Group campus specializing in doctoral programs in business and education, the average age of students is 41.

Given such diversity, it is risky to generalize about the students who attend for-profit colleges and universities. Overall demographic information on these students is sketchy, especially because the rise of the new for-profit universities is a relatively recent phenomenon and data gathered and reported by the National Center for Education Statistics (NCES) have not yet fully caught up with this trend. Until very recently, for example, national data on students attending proprietary institutions were lumped together by the NCES with data on community and junior colleges. The U.S. Department of Education published its first comprehensive statistical report on students attending for-profit institutions in 1999, but the data contained in this report pertained only to the 1993–94 and 1995–96 academic years and focus primarily on students attending less-than-four-year institutions.[1] Much of the growth in the for-profit sector has occurred since 1995, and it may be several more years before the national database provides more useful and current information.

Despite these limitations, however, I want to draw a composite picture, based on the available national data and also on information provided by some of the for-profit providers themselves, of the kind of student attending a four-year, for-profit university. Having made site visits to several of the campuses of the leading for-profit providers, where

I sat in on classes and talked with students, I will also draw upon my own firsthand observations.

The DOE published a study on nontraditional undergraduates in 1996 that provides some useful distinctions between the kinds of students attending public, private, and for-profit universities.[2] Table 2.2 provides a summary of some of these distinctions and also indicates the trends over the years.

Table 2.2   Selected Characteristics of Undergraduates at Public, Private, and For-Profit Colleges and Universities

	1986	1989	1992
Older than typical undergraduates[a]			
Public	57.0	59.1	61.5
Private	36.2	37.0	43.4
For-Profit	70.3	74.3	76.4
Independent undergraduates[b]			
Public	48.7	50.5	49.0
Private	31.5	32.7	37.6
For-Profit	61.8	68.7	68.3
Undergraduates with dependents[c]			
Public	20.9	22.8	19.9
Private	12.1	13.3	14.8
For-Profit	31.9	37.9	36.2
Single parent undergraduates			
Public	6.3	6.7	6.4
Private	3.6	3.9	4.7
For-Profit	18.0	21.6	19.4

Source: L. Horn and D. Carroll, *Nontraditional Undergraduates: Trends in Enrollment from 1986 to 1992 and Persistence and Attainment among 1989–90 Beginning Postsecondary Students,* U.S. Department of Education, National Center for Education Statistics, Statistical Analysis Report NCES 97-578 (November 1996).
[a]Students aged 20 or older their first year, 21 or older their second year, 22 or older their third year, or anyone 23 or older.
[b]Undergraduates who are determined to be financially independent for financial-aid purposes.
[c]Dependents other than a spouse.

As indicated by these data, students attending for-profit institutions are older than those attending non-profit institutions. The 1999 NCES report confirms these earlier findings, showing that in 1995–96, 40 percent of the students attending four-year, for-profit institutions were 30 years of age or older, up from 30 percent in 1991–92.[3] My sense is that more than 50 percent of the students attending for-profit institutions today are 30 or older, with another 30 percent 18–23 years old and the remaining 20 percent 24–29 years old. Table 2.2 also shows that compared with students attending traditional public and private institutions, a higher proportion of students attending the for-profits are financially independent, have dependents other than a spouse, and are single parents.

The for-profits also tend to attract a higher proportion of women and minority students. Of the top 100 institutions conferring degrees to people of color in 1988, proprietary colleges were major providers. The journal *Black Issues in Higher Education* reported in 1998 that the top producers of minority baccalaureates in engineering-related technologies and in computer and information sciences were for-profit institutions.[4] At my DeVry campus in New Jersey, more than 40 percent of the students are African American (the highest percentage at any New Jersey institution). About 43 percent of the students enrolled at Strayer University campuses are African American. Hispanics make up 8 percent of students attending four-year, for-profit colleges in the 1991–92 NCES report (compared with 5% in non-profit institutions), and this proportion had grown to 18 percent by 1995–96 (compared with 8% in the non-profits). In 1991–92 women accounted for 53 percent of the for-profit enrollment (67% in less-than-four-year, for-profit institutions), compared with 47 percent of the non-profit enrollment. (Why a higher proportion of minority students attend for-profit institutions is considered in chapter 3.)

The majority of students attending for-profit universities are also employed thirty-five or more hours per week. The NCES data show that 58 percent met these criteria in 1995–96, up from 50 percent in 1991–92. Based on my site visits to campuses of the five major for-profit providers profiled in this book, I would estimate that approximately two-thirds of their students were employed thirty-five or more hours per week in 1999–2000, compared with about one-third of the students in non-profit institutions. NCES also reported that a high proportion of students attending for-profit institutions delayed going to college after high school by at least one year, 46 percent in 1991–92, and 47 percent in 1995–96.

An NCES report released in March 2000 indicates that nearly half of the undergraduates attending for-profit institutions in 1995–96 were classified as low-income, compared with 21–26 percent attending non-profit institutions.[5]

In summary, a typical student pursuing a degree at a for-profit university fits the following demographic profile: 27-year-old female, ethnic minority (African American, Hispanic, or Asian), U.S. citizen, married, with one or two dependents, holding a full- or part-time job while going to school full time, and having some prior college experience. This student did not excel academically in high school and had mixed success in prior college work but has come to the realization that a college degree is the most sensible and effective route to a better job, a higher standard of living, and opportunities for career advancement. She is motivated and serious about education for perhaps the first time in her life. She sees higher education as a means to an end—a practical step toward a better future, greater economic security, and more options in life. In pursuing her degree, she is struggling to juggle the responsibilities of school, work, and family. How long this will take, how much she will have to sacrifice to achieve this goal, and how much it will cost are all vital questions for her. She is financing her education the same way most students do, through a combination of financial aid-grants and loans and personal savings.

Let me now provide a guided tour of the five major for-profit institutions, beginning with the two that stand out from the others in terms of their educational focus and degree programs: Education Management Corporation and Argosy Education Group.

Education Management Corporation

On Chestnut Street in downtown Philadelphia, surrounded by a variety of shops and cafes, the Art Institute of Philadelphia occupies a distinctive eight-story art deco building that was designed in 1928 to house CBS radio. The building has been designated by the Philadelphia Historical Commission as a historical site, and the exterior is itself a striking work of art. Remnants of the original art deco design are also preserved inside the building, around elevators and stairwells. The large entrance lobby also serves as a gallery, where institute faculty and students and other artists exhibit their work.

The impression upon entering the building is one of both an office building housing some business enterprise, with a formal reception area and controlled access to the upper floors, and an art gallery, with works exhibited along both sides of the large, open lobby, including a small table with brochures describing the artist and his or her work. On the day I visited the Art Institute of Philadelphia the gallery was displaying about 75 framed black-and-white photographs, organized as a retrospective of the work of a full-time faculty member.

Upstairs, the building looks more like an educational facility. It has the worn feeling of a 70-year-old, big-city office building that has endured a number of internal renovations. What is particularly striking is the display of student and faculty work. Glass display cases line many of the hallways and are full of photographs, drawings, models, paintings, and computer-generated graphics, all produced by students during the previous academic quarter and selected by the faculty as exemplary. More representative of the informal, relaxed culture of the institute, however, are all the works in progress taped to walls in classrooms, sketched on white boards, pinned up in doorways, hung up to dry in the darkrooms, and propped against work stations. The entire building, from the faculty offices to the television studios and the computer-animation labs, is a constantly changing gallery of works in progress. The instructional spaces themselves are diverse, ranging from traditional figure-drawing studios, with wooden easels and a posing platform for live models, to video-production rooms, 14 well-equipped computer labs, and traditional lecture-discussion classrooms with tablet armchairs.

Enrolling 2,500 students, the Art Institute of Philadelphia was founded by the artist Philip Trachtman in 1971 and acquired by Education Management Corporation in 1979. The institute has an open admissions policy, requiring proof of high-school graduation, an application essay, and an interview. The average age of the students is 23. Tuition in 2000 was $4,125 per quarter. Degree programs are offered at the associate and baccalaureate levels in graphic design, computer animation, interior design, industrial design technology, photography, multimedia and web design, and video production, as well as fashion marketing, fashion design, and, in a nearby facility, culinary arts.

Unlike most other art schools, the institute does not require a portfolio for admission. Instead, the development of a professional portfolio is an educational objective for each student before graduation. In its mission statement, the institute is clear that its purpose is to prepare students for entry-level employment in the career fields of the commercial arts. Average class size is 18, with the largest classes at about 30 and the studio classes at about 12 students. About 40 percent of the students complete their degree program. The job-placement rate is about 90 percent within six months of graduation. Average starting salaries are modest—about $25,000 for the associate's degree and just over $30,000 for the bachelor's degree.

Surrounded by five other art schools in or near downtown Philadelphia, the institute has developed a precise sense of its place in relation to the competition. The president of the Art Institute of Philadelphia, Stacey Sauchek, makes no pretense about the kind of student the institute serves. "I know about motivating and working with students who have learning difficulties," she told me, referring to her own background in school psychology, including a Ph.D. dissertation on aggressive student behavior.[6] She acknowledges that while a small proportion of her students already have bachelor's and master's degrees, the majority have not had a "stellar academic past." Regarding the more elite art programs that surround her campus, she noted, "There will always be money, people, and other resources devoted to working with students who are the cream of the crop. But, what about all the people in the middle? What about all the people who have been below average academically?"

Herein lies the particular mission of the Art Institute of Philadelphia: to enroll students with creative ability who may have a lackluster academic track record but are highly motivated to acquire the skills and the college degree they need in order to practice their vocation. Across higher education, many faculty desire to work with the best students, said Sauchek, but those who can work successfully with these kinds of students are accomplishing something noble. "In many cases," she said, "this is the first opportunity in a school setting where these students can really be successful."

The students I observed and talked with at the Art Institute of Philadelphia seemed to have a strong sense of community and friendship with other students. When I asked about this, Sauchek explained that "many of these students have been, educationally and even socially, the odd man out, the person with tattoos, perhaps in the fringe group socially in their high school. They come here and discover that they are not unlike many other highly creative people." Indeed, walking around the building, I could not help but notice that the tattoo and piercing quotient was high. I also could see students who went about their work seriously and with a sense of purpose, working on projects that, for them, are perhaps as much personal artistic expressions as they are class assignments. Many of the institute's students spend hours in the studios and labs beyond the time required for their classes. Some spend all day at the institute, grabbing a sandwich while working on a color-scheme assignment, occasionally stepping out to the front of the building for a cigarette.

"My philosophy," said Sauchek, "is that if you want to have an open door, that's fine, but then it is not fair to just let the students flounder, when you know they don't necessarily have the skills they need to succeed academically." She spoke sentimentally about the institute's graduation ceremonies, in which many students and family members celebrate with enthusiasm the first person in the family to earn an associate's degree. To provide academic and social support, the institute has a well-developed student-support system, with peer tutoring and a professional academic adviser assigned to each student. The director of student services, who manages the student-advising program, told me that he and his staff see about 150 students a week during a typical quarter. Eight members of the faculty serve as academic program directors and also devote a considerable amount of time to advising students.

The faculty of the Art Institute of Philadelphia includes 75 full-time and about 120 part-time members. Almost all of them are professional artists, consultants, and practitioners; most holding a master's degree, a few have a Ph.D., and a small group of the core art and design faculty hold no advanced degree. Teaching loads are relatively heavy, at 20 contact hours per week plus 4 office hours, with most faculty teaching five 4-hour classes each week. The faculty do not have tenure but are unionized, with contract negotiations every three years.

The Art Institute of Philadelphia is one of 16 campuses of the Art Institutes International, a wholly owned subsidiary of the Education Management Corporation, headquartered in Pittsburgh. Eight of the art institutes hold regional accreditation, and the others are in the process of gaining it. In addition to the art institutes, which form the company's core business, Education Management also owns the New York Restaurant School and the National Center for Paralegal Training. In 2000 the company's educational system included 20 campuses in 17 cities, with a total enrollment of about 25,000 students and about 3,000 employees. Systemwide, 46 percent of the faculty are full time, 54 percent part time. Currently, degree programs are offered only at the undergraduate level.

Founded in 1962, Education Management went public in 1996. Three years later the value of the company's stock had increased by 269 percent. Headed by Robert Knutson, chairman and CEO, the company was ranked 56th among Forbes Best 200 Small Companies in 1999. The corporate growth strategy includes opening two new campuses each year, through either acquisition or start up.

Most of the growth in recent years has in fact been through acquisition. In 1997, for example, the company purchased a majority share in the Salinger School, in San Francisco, which it renamed the Art Institutes International at San Francisco. Similarly, in 1998 it acquired Bassist College in Portland, Oregon, and renamed it the Art Institutes International at Portland. Most recently, the company acquired Massachusetts Communications College in Boston and the American Business and Fashion Institute in Charlotte, North Carolina.

Argosy Education Group

With its emphasis on doctoral-level education through the American Schools of Professional Psychology (ASPP), the faculty culture at Argosy resembles that of many non-profit graduate schools in several respects. The faculty handbook, for example, contains strong statements about collegiality and academic freedom, and the significant role of the faculty in governance is clearly spelled out. The full-time faculty in the ASPP (85 members, plus another 166 adjuncts, all of whom are doctorally qualified) are directly involved in admissions decisions, faculty review and evaluation, all curricular matters, library acquisitions, and faculty recruiting and hiring. The academic voice at the top of the company is strong, which is not typical of most of the for-profit providers organized as publicly traded companies. Both Argosy's chairman, Michael Markovitz, and the provost, Jack Sites, were trained as academicians. "We are educators in the business of education," Markovitz asserts, "not business people selling education."[7]

Yet there are also striking differences between Argosy's academic culture and that of a traditional non-profit university. For example, faculty are required to be on campus four eight-hour days each week during the semesters, and the clinical faculty must devote the fifth day to clinical practice. No tenure system exists; faculty are offered two- or three-year renewable contracts. Teaching loads typically involve six course sections a year, plus two doctoral seminars. In addition, faculty serve as clinical mentors of groups of students. Faculty salaries are reasonably good but not great, somewhere in the range of the 40th to 45th percentile on the annual salary data published by the American Psychological Association. Most, if not all, of the ASPP faculty also have active clinical or consulting practices, since clinical work is a requirement for the faculty who teach clinical courses and is encouraged for others. Eli Schwartz, a faculty member, former academic dean, and now assistant to the provost, stated, "I want my abnormal-psychology instructors to be involved in diagnostic work. I tell them, 'That's what we pay you for, not for publications.'"[8]

The lack of emphasis on scholarly publication is a reflection of Argosy's philosophy of the Psy.D. degree. The Psy.D. movement within clinical psychology began about 30 years ago within the American Psychological Association, and by the 1990s the Psy.D. had established itself as a legitimate and desired credential for clinical practitioners. In 1992 there were 37 Psy.D. programs in the United States. By 1997 there were 55. Advocates of the Psy.D. draw parallels to the fields of medicine and law, pointing out that physicians earn M.D.'s, not Ph.D.'s in biology, and lawyers earn J.D.'s, not Ph.D.'s in law. Unlike the Ph.D. in psychology, this is not a research degree but a clinical credential. The corpo-

rate leadership, academic deans, and the faculty at Argosy have culti-
vated a clear and sophisticated understanding of this difference and its
impact on the role of the faculty and the curriculum.

"A great deal of what we do pertains to the integration of knowledge," Schwartz told me, "with the goal of translating learning into the
reality of clinical situation." Being able to apply knowledge, he suggested, is perhaps a different kind of intelligence than being able to
demonstrate intellectual grasp in the classroom. "Even straight-A students are not necessarily savvy enough to know how to use human interaction to bring about change," said Schwartz. "Getting As is often a
reflection of good memory, but the hallmark of critical thinking is inte-
grating knowledge in a problem-solving situation." Schwartz believes
passionately that the best way to teach clinical skills, whether involving
human interaction or cutting into the body, is what he calls the "follow
me" principle, whereby the teaching faculty demonstrate clinical techniques by showing students how they do it.

The founder and current chairman is Michael Markovitz, a Ph.D.
psychologist who took action 25 years ago in response to the demand
for a non-research-oriented doctoral degree for practitioners in clinical
psychology. Recalling the process of founding the institution, Markovitz
said that at the time "there was no real sense that it was more noble to
be non-profit. The nobility lay in the execution of the idea."[9]

Argosy was founded in Chicago as the Illinois School of Professional
Psychology in 1975; the company went public in March 1999. *Business
Week* named Argosy one of 100 "hot growth companies" in May 2000.
Argosy is the largest provider of graduate education in psychology in
the county (graduating 360 doctoral students in 1998) and also the only
doctoral-level institution run by a for-profit corporation. Five of the
ten campuses of the ASPP hold accreditation at the doctoral level by
the American Psychological Association, and the other five are in readi-
ness for APA accreditation and will very likely gain it. Enrollment in
the ASPP schools is about 2,000 graduate students (62% of Argosy's
students are enrolled in doctoral programs, another 17% in master's
programs). Argosy's Psy.D. program is a four-year program with an annual tuition of about $13,000. Total enrollment in all of Argosy's opera-
tions was about 5,000 in 2000.

Part of Argosy's appeal as both an investment opportunity and an educational institution is its strong track record in taking over institutions on the brink of bankruptcy or of losing their accreditation, or both, and turning them around. This was the case with Argosy's acquisition in 1992 of the University of Sarasota, which had declared bankruptcy, was on the verge of losing both its Southern Association of Colleges and Schools (SACS) accreditation and its state license, and was enrolling fewer than 100 students. Argosy guided the University of Sarasota through a remarkable transformation, bringing enrollments to over 2,000 in 1999, expanding and deepening the curricula, and maintaining full accreditation from SACS.

In 1999 Argosy took over the John Marshall Law School, in Atlanta, Georgia, becoming the first for-profit provider to offer doctoral-level education in law. The 68-year-old law school had operated since its founding under the direct approval of the Georgia Supreme Court without accreditation by the American Bar Association. In 1987 the court ruled that the school must either attain ABA accreditation by 2003 or close its doors. Argosy entered the picture on a contract basis to run the John Marshall Law School under a 10-year purchase option on the school. Having now completed the ABA accreditation process ahead of schedule (Argosy officials said the exit interview went very well), the school is awaiting final word from the ABA.

Argosy has acquired 8 of its 17 campuses, 4 of which were originally non-profit institutions. Aside from the University of Sarasota and the John Marshall Law School, other acquisitions include the Medical Institute of Minnesota, which offers associate degrees in several allied health fields and is accredited by the Accrediting Bureau of Health Education Schools; Prime-Tech Institute, which offers Canadian diplomas in information technology fields at three Canadian campuses; and the Ventura Group, a provider of licensing-examination preparation courses in the fields of psychology, social work, and counseling.

DeVry Institute of Technology

Located right off busy U.S. Highway One amid corporate office buildings and just a few miles from the Rutgers University campus stands the handsome, no-frills building that houses the New Jersey campus of DeVry Institute of Technology. A huge asphalt parking lot surrounds the 110,000-square-foot glass and steel structure, and on weekdays the lot is nearly full from 7:00 A.M. to 10:30 P.M. Out front, American and New Jersey state flags fly on 100-foot flagpoles, and the small green areas around the building sprout young trees and the well-trimmed landscaping typical of corporate facilities located on the outskirts of U.S. cities.

One of 19 DeVry campuses—there are 16 in the United States and in Canada—the New Jersey facility is typical. Walking in the front entrance, one is immediately struck by how much the building looks and feels like an office complex rather than a typical educational institution. The entrance lobby is lined with reproductions of modern abstract art, potted plants, and large, framed copies of DeVry's mission statement, statement of purposes, and philosophy of general education. A professional receptionist sits behind a glass enclosure, flanked by video monitors announcing the day's events. Several people wearing dark business suits (admissions representatives) scurry by, while a small group in shirtsleeves and pocket protectors (members of the technical faculty) stroll by. Students wearing backpacks and carrying what look like fishing tackle boxes, which are actually electronics lab kits containing circuit boards and other components, head off to class. The place is very busy.

Calling the building a "campus" seems a bit of a stretch since everything from classrooms and labs to faculty offices, the library, the registrar's office, student services, the president's office, and the cafeteria are all housed in this one building. There are no student residences, although about 300 students live in nearby apartment complexes subleased to DeVry. A model of efficiency, the campus building is DeVry's blueprint for its Institutes of Technology, designed to house about 80 full-time faculty, enroll 3,700 students, and run classes six or seven days a week from early in the morning to late at night. The 20-plus classrooms hold about 40 students each and are well equipped with video monitors, computer projectors, and white boards; some have tables and chairs with hookups so that each student can use a laptop PC. Laboratories to support programs in telecommunications, electronics-engineering technology, and business information systems are interspersed throughout the building. The largest PC lab has 150 work stations, the smallest about 30. Most of the computer equipment is brand-new or less than 18 months old.

A two-story library in the center of the building opens to skylights at the top, and most of the seats are taken by studying students. Bowing to pressure from regional association accrediting teams, DeVry has for several years allocated increasingly more money to build its library collection and facilities. This one holds about 30,000 volumes, plus several thousand electronic books, and a well-developed network of online resources served by 25 work stations and available through remote access. Only five years ago, however, the typical DeVry library housed only about 10,000 volumes, including some materials that probably should have been discarded long ago. Back then the libraries got the older, hand-me-down computers.

Investing in traditional, books-on-the-shelf libraries is a hard sell at DeVry (and in the for-profit sector generally), where corporate finance officers find it difficult to see the return on such an investment. Investing in new computer equipment, on the other hand, is an easy sell since DeVry graduates have to be familiar with current hardware and software applications in order to be placed in good jobs. Libraries are basically regarded as an expensive and somewhat marginal utility, especially since a good proportion of DeVry students (and, it must be said, some of the technical faculty) do not avail themselves of the libraries' resources. Were it not for a clear directive from the North Central Association, which currently provides regional accreditation for all of DeVry's U.S. campuses, the corporate leadership at DeVry probably would have been satisfied with smaller libraries.

Signs of both the old DeVry, which has been around since the 1930s, and the new DeVry, which has flourished with the revolution in information technology, are apparent on this campus. The old DeVry can be seen in the electronics lab, which despite the recent addition of PCs at each work station looks like a throwback to the time of transistors and soldering guns. Here students sit on stools and lean over benches to assemble various kinds of circuits and then troubleshoot using voltage meters and oscillators. The pocket-protector quotient is high in this environment. Throughout most of its 70-year history this kind of instruction was DeVry's core business, and though the market has shifted somewhat, each new campus—at least two are built each year—includes a sizable electronics lab. During the 1990s, enrollment in the electronics programs leveled off and declined somewhat in favor of the newer offerings in telecommunications and information systems. In response, in 1999 the New Jersey campus downsized its electronics lab and reallocated space in order to expand the telecommunications lab. The new DeVry is evident in the telecommunications lab, where students labor at new PC work stations to design and operate local and wide area networks and create simulations of various transmission media, such as fiber optics and wireless.

The 74 full-time faculty at the New Jersey campus are paired in 12-by-10-foot offices with desks, bookshelves, filing cabinets, PCs, and a printer. The faculty office area is modest and professional, with no cartoons or other material posted on office doors (this is against company policy, unwritten but strictly enforced). All of the faculty are issued new laptop computers, which they are encouraged and trained to use in the classrooms. About one-third have doctoral degrees, and the rest have master's degrees and significant experience in industry. Teaching loads are targeted at 15 hours a semester (generally three to five courses per week), with three semesters running year round. Some have modest release time for duties as department chairpersons and for curriculum development. A handful are given release time for Ph.D. work, especially those at the dissertation stage. One-semester sabbaticals are available every five years. DeVry also reimburses full-time faculty for doctoral-level coursework, up to $5,000 annually. Faculty salaries average just over $50,000 annually, with the lower salaries (ca. $45,000) in general education and the higher salaries (ca. $65,000) in the technical fields. Several of the full-time faculty teach an additional evening or weekend course each semester, adding another $10,000 to $20,000 to their annual base salary.

Two aspects of the allocation of human resources at DeVry are noteworthy. First, the admissions office employs a staff of about 30 full-time employees plus another 7 field representatives who visit high schools, which is a large staff for a campus of only 3,500 students. Second, the placement office is also relatively large, with about 13 full-time employees. Together, these two offices represent DeVry's sales force, the first focused on selling prospective students and the second focused on selling employers to hire DeVry graduates. Both operations are businesslike and successful, with admissions bringing in larger freshmen classes in each of the past five years and the placement office achieving a 95 percent placement rate for ten years running. From a business standpoint, the admissions and placement functions are the engines of DeVry's financial success. Growth in admissions assures growth in revenues, and the high placement rate drives the whole enterprise.

As a system, DeVry enrolls about 50,000 students and has been sustaining double-digit enrollment growth each year since the company went public in 1991. In 2000 DeVry was ranked 11th on *Business Ethics's* "100 Best Corporate Citizens" list—a ranking of public companies based on how well they serve employees, customers, the community, and stockholders—up from a ranking of 77th in 1996. DeVry's corporate growth strategy is to open two new campuses each year for the next ten years and also to keep an eye out for acquisitions that meet the criteria of established brand name, strong market presence, and clear growth potential. Denver Technical College met those criteria and was acquired in 1999. DeVry, Inc., is the holding company for DeVry University, comprising the 19 DeVry campuses plus the 35 sites of the Keller Graduate School of Management, which enrolls about 6,000 students in six different master's degree programs, all available online. DeVry, Inc., also includes the Becker Conviser CPA Review, the largest accounting-examination review course, taught on four continents and serving about 32,000 students annually.

Founded in 1931 in Chicago, DeVry grew out of the pioneering work of Dr. Herman DeVry, an inventor and teacher at Bell & Howell, which in the 1930s was the equivalent of today's cutting-edge high-tech companies. Responding to the growing need for training in electronics resulting from the rapid development of consumer technology and products, Herman DeVry brought Bell & Howell into the education business. DeVry institutes were set up in several cities and flourished until the 1970s, when the demand for such training began to wane.

Two enterprising businessmen, Dennis Keller, a Princeton graduate with an M.B.A. from Chicago, and Ron Taylor, a Harvard graduate with an M.B.A. from Stanford, bought the DeVry operation from Bell & Howell in 1987. Keller is the chairman and CEO, Taylor the president and COO, and each is highly skilled in his own way. Keller is the visionary leader, with a mellifluous baritone voice and an unflappably positive attitude. Taylor is the tough drill sergeant who keeps the pressure on everyone to deliver results. Wall Street analysts consider Keller and Taylor to be one of the strongest management teams in the industry. As we will see in chapter 4, the numbers certainly bear this out.

Strayer University

White Marsh, Maryland, is a bedroom community of Baltimore with sprawling shopping malls, outlet centers, condominiums, industrial parks, and dozens of new construction projects underway. Except in the old section of White Marsh, most of the architecture is new, and the whole area is zoned for the kind of prosperity that only a booming economy can support. Traffic is heavy and continuous, with commuters and shoppers flowing in and out on I-95 and the Beltway. In a new, one-story brick-and-stucco building on Philadelphia Avenue sits the 13th and newest campus of Strayer University. Its 17 classrooms and computer labs are equipped with new furniture and hardware, awaiting the steady, incremental enrollment growth that Strayer has come to expect with its careful, deliberate expansion along the Washington-Baltimore corridor. The first class at White Marsh had 107 students, slightly ahead of projection, and John Shufold, the campus dean, expects enrollments to grow to over 300 by the start of the next quarter.

Dean Shufold is concerned, however, that prospective students be carefully advised about which of Strayer's programs they should choose, and so he tries to see as many of them as possible himself in order to guide them in the right curricular direction.[10] Like most for-profit deans, he is under pressure to improve student retention and completion rates. The current hot program at Strayer is the B.S. in computer information systems and computer networking, and while it is an easy sell for the admissions representatives, he believes that some students who enter this program do not have the aptitude and skills needed to get through the curriculum successfully.

Tension between the academic side of the house and admissions (read "sales") is common in the for-profit providers, especially at institutions like Strayer, which have an essentially open admissions policy. Programs in computers and technology are extremely attractive to potential students who lack such backgrounds, but the curricula are fairly demanding, requiring basic skills in algebra and calculus, and some students are simply not prepared to handle the rigor of the subject matter. Yet, about 40 percent of Strayer's students make it through to graduation, and the company does not want to deny them this opportunity.

Founded in 1892 as Strayer's Business College of Baltimore City, Strayer University has the longest history of continuous operation among the for-profit providers profiled in this chapter and is also one the smallest, with about 12,500 students enrolled in 2000. Strayer's 13 campuses are located in Maryland, Virginia, and Washington, D.C., offering programs in computer information systems and business at the associate's, bachelor's, and master's levels. About one-third of the 300 faculty are full time.

Consistent with a strategy of targeting its programs to older, employed students, more than 60 percent of Strayer's students are over 30 years old and the majority study part time. African Americans account for 42 percent of the student body, and 55 percent of the students are women. "We think we fill a niche that others are not meeting," Harry Wilkins, Strayer's chief financial officer, told me, "and that is providing an education targeted to working adults."[11] He went on to describe Strayer's target market as "students who make it through the secondary educational system but emerge undereducated and uninspired by their educational experience and don't go on to college until they reach their thirties." Working adults, said Wilkins, often want an education that prepares them for certification in Oracle and Java programming and Microsoft networking. They do not particularly want to sit in community-college classrooms with 18- and 19-year-olds. "If they go to a traditional education institution," Wilkins observed, "they tend to get the same kind of experience they did not like in high school." What Strayer seeks to provide is a highly structured learning experience with an emphasis on personal attention.

Strayer gained accreditation from Middle States in 1981 and went public in July 1996. *Forbes* selected Strayer as among the 200 best small companies in 1999, and *Business Week* selected it as among the 200 best small companies in America in 1998. This kind of recognition appeals to the adult student population Strayer serves. While Strayer's name (or the name of any of the for-profits, for that matter) does not appear on the lists of college and university rankings provided by *U.S. News & World Report* and *Money* magazine, it has been recognized as an effective and well-managed enterprise. The academic leaders I talked to at Strayer suggested that the kinds of students they attract place a high value on having a professional and businesslike relationship with their educational provider and are less concerned about the conventional academic rankings.

Wilkins observed that some prestigious non-profit institutions behave as if the value of their services is based on their ability to restrict access to only certain kinds of students. Wilkins himself is a graduate of Loyola College in Maryland and served on the advisory board of its business school. He said, "The admissions director would be proud to announce in our meetings that we had 12,000 applicants and we were only taking 3,000 incoming freshmen." In contrast, Strayer's success is based on providing educational access to adult students who are underserved by many non-profit colleges and universities.

Apollo Group

"The flagship campus of the University of Phoenix," writes Arthur Padilla, "doesn't look like any typical university. Its unprepossessing entrance is difficult to find, beyond waving banners of car dealerships and a variety of one-story offices and businesses."[12] Arriving during the daytime, Padilla, a management professor at North Carolina State University, discovered a near-empty parking lot and no students. Inside, there was no student center and no library, just a small snack bar and a little bookstore. "Visitors may have difficulty understanding why this institution has generated so much discussion nationally," he notes.

The big deal about the University of Phoenix is not its campus facilities. "Whatever you do," warns an article in *University Business,* "it would be risky to ignore the Phoenix phenomenon."[13] Indeed, the phenomenal growth of the largest of the nation's private universities (whether non-profit or for-profit) is almost impossible to ignore. Attempts to dismiss the University of Phoenix as a kind of error, perhaps the academic equivalent of a stock-market correction (as the provost of a large state university recently suggested to me), are too often based on a combination of misinformation and wishful thinking.

The sheer size of the enterprise alone is intimidating, with an enrollment of more than 100,000 students whose average age is 35 and whose average annual income is $56,000. Nearly two-thirds of its students are women. The Apollo Group, the publicly traded holding company that owns the University of Phoenix, has grown so vigorously that even the Internet investment sites have not kept up with the business expansion. One hundred thousand students is nothing to sniff at and cannot be written off as simply a large case of misinformed student consumers. Clearly, the University of Phoenix appeals to adult working professionals who have reached a certain level of success in their careers and are probably fairly savvy educational consumers. Referring to the notion held by some accreditors and state licensing agencies that adult student consumers actually need several layers of regulatory protection against unscrupulous colleges and universities, John G. Sperling, the founder and CEO of Apollo, says, "They also believe that consumers of educational services—even intelligent, well-educated adults—cannot adequately judge the value of the services they receive."[14]

It is difficult not to interpret Phoenix's aggressive growth and continued expansion as a threat to traditional higher education, and yet it is too easy to dismiss the Phoenix phenomenon as "Drive-Thru U" and "McEducation." The essential threat is not so much that Phoenix is taking away market share, for when a Phoenix campus enters a local market, it tends to generate additional enrollment gains in neighboring community colleges and general education programs.[15] What is threatening about the University of Phoenix is that it represents radical change in higher education.

"Phoenix heralds a potential revolution in higher education," says Arthur Levine, president of Teachers College at Columbia University.[16] Sperling, Phoenix's irascible founder and CEO, is often portrayed as the Clint Eastwood of higher education (armed with a Ph.D. from Cambridge University), arriving in town during the night, daring you to meet him in the street at noon to make his day. Indeed, unlike DeVry, Strayer, Argosy, and Education Management, which are quite content to inquire of accrediting bodies and state licensing agencies, "Tell us what the rules are and we will play by them," the Phoenix approach has been more like, "The rules have changed and you need to wake up." By sheer force of will, business acumen, and a ready multitude of students, the University of Phoenix has apparently ushered in a new era in American higher education.

The Phoenix story is essentially one of aggressive growth brought about by giving the education marketplace what it wants and then continuing to push the edges of that growth by harnessing the resources of a well-capitalized corporation. There are any number of ways to measure Phoenix's growth—enrollments, campus locations, revenue, assessment of outcomes, return to stockholders—and all of them show impressive results. A quick measure is provided by the growth in the value of Apollo's stock, which increased by 1,538 percent between 1994, the year the company went public, and 1999. That kind of growth gets attention and attracts investors, and it is no small irony that among Apollo's top 25 institutional investors is the venerable TIAA-CREF, the retirement-annuity provider for faculty members at non-profit colleges and universities all across America. Millions of faculty members at non-profit institutions are investing in the success of the University of Phoenix through their retirement fund contributions to TIAA-CREF.

Apollo Group's revenues amounted to $500 million in 1999, its fifth year of operation as a public company and the University of Phoenix's forty-fourth year of operations. Phoenix gained North Central Association accreditation in 1978, its nursing program is accredited at the baccalaureate and master's levels by the National League of Nursing Accreditation Commission, and its master's program in community counseling is accredited by the Council for Accreditation of Counseling and Related Educational Programs Commission. Degree programs include associate's and bachelor's-degrees in business, management, information systems, accounting, information technology, and nursing and master's-degree programs in business, health-care management, nursing, education, counseling, and computer information systems. The Apollo system includes 52 campuses and 85 learning centers that function as satellite campuses. Tuition at the University of Phoenix is about $8,000 a year, and about 80 percent of the students receive tuition reimbursement from their employers.

More than 5,000 instructors work for Apollo, and all but about 150 are part time, earning from $1,500 to $2,500 per five-week course. Apollo also reimburses faculty for travel expenses to and from classes and pays them a stipend for attending faculty meetings. The company also provides travel funds for part-time faculty to attend academic conferences and professional meetings. All new faculty go through a 20-hour training program.

The public academic voice of the University of Phoenix is Jorge de

Alva, the university's president. De Alva is an erudite scholar and consummate debater who, after achieving the rank of full professor in anthropology at Princeton, followed by an endowed chair at Berkeley, has now made the University of Phoenix the focus of his intellectual passion. De Alva was successful in terms of all of the standard measures academic success—NEH and NSF grants, a Guggenheim Fellowship, a Getty Scholarship, a Fulbright Scholarship, and 24 scholarly books—and it is difficult to dismiss him as a businessman who does not understand academia.

"If you look at the history of higher education in the West," he says, "it began pretty much as a for-profit affair. In fact, the University of Phoenix's roots are not outside of the academy, any more than Protestantism is outside of traditional Christianity."[17] To the question whether the University of Phoenix is serving society or merely generating profits, De Alva replies, "We are educating tens of thousands of students at no taxpayer's expense and returning a significant portion of our revenues back into the economy for other uses." By "returning a significant portion of revenues" he is referring to the for-profit providers' payment of income taxes at the rate of approximately 40 percent earnings before taxes, through which they return more to the public treasury than they receive in the form of federally insured loan subsidies for their students.[18]

The Phoenix phenomenon follows a simple and powerful logic, aligned with ideals less familiar to non-profit higher education than to the world of commerce and the market economy. Jorge de Alva explains it this way: "We seek to increase the productivity of individual students, who in turn increase the productivity of companies, which in turn increase the productivity of regions, which ultimately generates no small part of the tax base that helps people give to the endowments of non-profit universities."

Indeed, the endowment funds of at least two non-profit universities have benefited directly from the success of one of the for-profit providers, DeVry, Inc. Dennis Keller, DeVry's chairman and CEO, gave $25 million to the University of Chicago in 1999 and $20 million to Princeton University in 1997. (A more thorough consideration of the impact of the University of Phoenix and other for-profit institutions on the higher-education industry is presented in chapter 6.)

3

The History of For-Profit Education
in the United States

The Origins of For-Profit Education

"But a very small proportion can be of the so-called learned professions," reads a letter to the editor published in the *Boston Transcript* in
1873, "and most of us must be of the productive, toiling class." The
fundamental problem was that many of America's skilled workers, "ma-
chinists, miners, weavers, watchmakers, iron-workers, draftsmen, and
artisans of every description, come from abroad."[1] The director of the
newly founded Manual Training School, in St. Louis, in an address on
the campus the same year summarized the situation as follows: "Every
young man (and perhaps every young woman, too) should receive special theoretical and practical training in some one respectable trade or
profession. . . . Parents and business men are of the opinion, secret
perhaps, but firmly held, that higher education oftener *unfits* than *fits*
a man for earning a living."[2]

Fueled by the market demand for applications-oriented education,
the predecessors of today's for-profit schools were focused on prepar-

ing young men and women for entry into, and advancement in, a rapidly changing society, economy, and job market. This focus is the same today as it was in the nineteenth century, perhaps even more so given the advent of the so-called knowledge-based economy of the twenty-first century, which has created continuing demand for a well-educated and skillfully trained work force.

It is one thing to call yourself a manual training school and not offer college degrees, not seek regional accreditation, and stay in your place by simply meeting the demand for a rather pedestrian form of education. It is quite another to call yourself a university, attract billions of dollars of private investment capital, gain unexpected academic legitimacy, threaten to take away market share from traditional institutions, and even be held up as a model by some people of how a university ought to be run.

The new level of legitimacy that the for-profit university attained during the decade of the 1990s came about through the creation and rapid growth of large, publicly traded corporations that own and run multicampus universities. In stark contrast to the family-owned, mom-and-pop, storefront proprietary schools, these well-capitalized corporations listed on the stock exchange have built campuses that are at once both bare-bones and state-of-the-art, created around curricula in high demand by both students and employers. Ownership of these companies is not held by proprietors but is publicly traded through the sale of stock, which is held by hundreds of thousands of private citizens. Owned by the public and run by professional managers, these institutions are a new breed of publicly held university, providing education at no cost to taxpayers and offering the full complement of federal financial aid to students. They have taken a traditional model of learning—students seated in classrooms with a professor up front—and run it like a business.

These corporations are a relatively new development in American higher education, and it may seem as if they came out of nowhere. In fact, they represent only the most recent development in the long and intriguing history of for-profit institutions of higher education in the United States. For as long as there has been a social and economic need for the acquisition of knowledge and the development of skills, enterprising individuals, groups, and organizations have found ways to provide education to meet these needs. An understanding of the nature of the modern for-profit universities is greatly enhanced by an appreciation of the historical context out of which they emerged.

Where the For-Profits Came From

Private education for a fee has its roots in the settlement of the American colonies. The first proprietary schools, like their modern successors, grew out of the entrepreneurial passion embedded in American culture and the free-market economy.

Surviving records indicate that by as early as 1660 Dutch settlers had well-established evening schools for the teaching of mathematics, reading, and writing.[3] Local masters (proprietors), usually trained as clergy, who made their living as teachers and tutors ran these private evening schools and served as the faculty. They were free to create such schools without any government approval or oversight. These schools, as described by the educational historian Robert Seybolt, became a prominent form of basic education and an important and popular feature of institutional life in colonial America.[4]

Responding to the interests of students, many of whom were adults, the curricula of these early schools soon expanded beyond mathematics, reading, and writing to include languages, particularly French, Italian, Portuguese, and Spanish.[5] As demand grew and changed, occupational programs were added to teach skills that were in high demand by employers, such as surveying, navigation, and bookkeeping, which in turn led to good jobs for graduates and increased opportunities for their social and economic advancement. Although there was a growing need for these skills in early American society, such subjects were not taught in the early colleges or the public "free schools."

Thus, educational and economic needs of the times were often met by individual entrepreneurs who offered to teach others their skills and knowledge for a fee. Their survival in these endeavors depended on their ability to keep abreast of changing social needs for specific types of education and training and to meet those needs to the satisfaction of both students and employers. Some of these schools were so successful that after a time they became formal colleges.

Lawrence Cremin, in his Pulitzer Prize–winning studies of colonial education, describes how human ingenuity and private enterprise flourished in colonial education, fueled by such forces as "cheap land, flourishing commerce, and a persistent scarcity of labor."[6] In the larger cities of Boston, New York, Philadelphia, and Charleston private teachers offered instruction to both children and adults in a variety of academic subjects, skilled trades, languages, and the polite arts of dancing, fencing, and needlework. One of the best-known private teachers in the colonies was George Brownell, who taught Benjamin Franklin writing and arithmetic after Franklin's father, Josiah, pulled Ben out of Latin school.[7]

Benjamin Franklin's influence on the development of early American education was significant in legitimizing the value of practical instruction in the business of living. When he founded his great educational experiment, the Public Academy, in the city of Philadelphia, Franklin envisioned an institution that would be grounded in practical and applied studies. This vision was hard won, and Franklin recalled at the end of his life that he had had constantly to fight the Latinists among his trustees and faculty, who lobbied for a more classical curriculum. In the end, he declared the experiment a failure, lamenting in his journal that some people seem to have "an unaccountable prejudice in favor of ancient customs and habitudes."[8]

Franklin himself was largely a product of self-education and the system of apprenticeship brought over from Europe by handicraftsman, artisans, and tradesmen. He helped to move the apprenticeship system into the curricula of the private schools, where the process was broadened and made more efficient. Instead of working with only one apprentice at a time, a master could work with a group of six or eight students. Study was broadened to include mathematical concepts and bits of theory, which the traditional apprenticeship instruction did not always include. Occupational training often coexisted in the curricula of these schools with the development of social skills and personal character.[9] Like Franklin's *Poor Richard's Almanack,* these schools sought to advance the "virtues of industry, frugality, and prudence in the conduct of life, the possibilities of power and station to be derived from the pursuit of one's calling, and the principles of utility and self-help in the quest for education."[10]

The Genteel Business of Education

When organized higher education first began to take shape in America, the early institutions themselves were unique blends of public, private, for-profit, and non-profit organizations. This blending of public, private, for-profit, and non-profit is recurring today in American higher education (see chapter 6). In colonial times, the division of organizational life into for-profit and non-profit, public and private, business and government, was not clear-cut. It was not unusual to run a school like a business. Church and state were interwoven and often indistinguishable.[11] Harvard College was chartered in 1650, but only two hundred years later did Harvard decide whether it was a private or a public institution.[12] Such profitable and private organizations as the Dutch West India Company were instrumental in providing financial support for both public and private educational ventures throughout the colonies.[13]

According to some educational historians, America already had, before the time of the American Revolution, a system of degree-granting academic institutions that was larger and more comprehensive than that of Great Britain.[14] This system was extremely diverse, just as it is today, with schools of every size, shape, and configuration, supported financially through a combination of fees, subscriptions, taxes, endowments, and private investments. What has been largely unacknowledged is that this educational system developed primarily as the result of private enterprise.[15]

The earliest formation and largest segment (in terms of numbers of institutions) of organized education in the United States was the independent proprietary school, run as a "genteel business" in order to support a scholar's family.[16] Like their modern successors, these schools were run on a proprietary basis and received no public financial support. The early proprietary schools and those that survived even as the country's public educational system developed, as well as those that are flourishing today, represent a uniquely American phenomena. "Nothing exactly like it is known in other countries," wrote educational historian Edmund James in 1900, noting that the for-profit commercial school "embodies all the defects and the excellencies of the American character."[17] Such defects and qualities of excellence still exist today in the modern for-profit university, in which the profit motive and a teaching mission sometimes struggle to peacefully coexist. More about this struggle later.

The Limitations of the Classical College

The for-profit sector of higher education continued to develop in part because of what was not provided by the traditional colleges and the English grammar school. Based on the British models of Cambridge and Oxford, the early American colleges devoted themselves almost exclusively to the teaching and study of theology, Greek and Latin languages, classical literature, and philosophy. While catering to the so-called learned professions of law, medicine, teaching, and the ministry, the classical colleges were not particularly concerned about addressing the educational needs in what Lawrence Cremin calls the "productive professions," such as business, farming, and engineering.[18] The clergy, who were generally the most highly educated class, strongly influenced the mission of these colleges, and the churches provided necessary financial support. The founding of Harvard (Puritans), William and Mary (Anglicans), Yale (Congregationalists), Princeton (Presbyterians), and Brown (Baptists) occurred under the philanthropic influence of organized religion. These institutions existed primarily to educate the sons of the leading families and to support the development of a cultured clergy and social class.[19]

Fulfilling the need for people knowledgeable about physical problems and skilled in solving them, such as surveyors for land development and navigators to guide ship traffic in and out of ports, was left mainly to private enterprise. The early for-profit schools responded to these needs in ways that were creative and effective. The role of private enterprise was a key component in providing students with options and alternatives for gaining education and training, for there was a disconnect between what the traditional colleges provided and what the market economy was demanding (and in my view this is still true). The distribution of books in the library collection at Harvard, for example, reveals this disconnect. In 1723, of the library's 2,961 titles, 58 percent were in theology, and only two books in the library were on the subject of commerce.[20] Harvard and its library were responding to a different kind of demand, namely, the need for an educated clergy. But the need for an educated clergy was only one of the many demands placed upon America's early educational system, and this of course in part explains the diversity of the developing system of education providers.

By the mid-nineteenth century, as the country began to gear up for rapid geographic and economic expansion, the rise of the new factory system, and emerging industrialization, there were critical needs for engineers, chemists, and manufacturers to help build and run new kinds of enterprises. These experts often had to be imported, at great expense, from Holland, England, Germany, and France. In 1899 Charles Dabney, president of the University of Tennessee, wrote: "A vigorous demand arose for the sciences and their applications to the arts of life. The old college was not meeting the new demands."[21]

It was not until after World War I that the first federal legislation, the Vocational Act of 1917, was enacted to provide support for what was called "career education," as opposed to purely academic instruction, even though the Morrill Act of 1862 had established funding for land-grant colleges in each state to promote education in agriculture and the "mechanic arts." Career education was not offered in the classical colleges, but as Arthur Bolino writes, it "survived in the evening schools, in private schools, in the extension and correspondence schools, and in the military because it provided a service that was unavailable elsewhere."[22]

The Example of Agricultural Education

Early agricultural educational institutions responded to these pragmatic social and economic needs. By the end of the eighteenth century a body of scientific knowledge had begun to develop in western Europe around the technology and chemistry of farming. In America, the first society for the promotion of agriculture in the United States was formed in Philadelphia in 1785, and several others had sprung up in New England by 1800. At meetings and agricultural fairs American farmers began to learn about the new application of science to farming, which eventually led to an increasing demand for scientific and technical education. Farmers and officials of agricultural societies turned to the colleges for help in addressing this demand, but as noted above, the colleges were focused on providing education for the so-called learned professions, not for farming.

The surveyor-general of New York is attributed with issuing the first call for "the necessity of establishing an agricultural college" in 1819, in response to the requests of many constituents.[23] Interest in and demand for such colleges continued to grow within the agricultural community, which at the time included the majority of American families. In New York in 1838, petitions bearing 6,000 signatures were presented to the legislature requesting state aid to create an agricultural school. Similar petitions were filed in other cities and states around the country.

The first agricultural college, however, was not established until 1855, at Michigan State University. It took fifty years to add agriculture to the college curriculum once the demand for such education became widely known. In the interim, many successful for-profit agricultural schools thrived.

In New York, one of the first of these was the Oneida Institute, which offered a program in practical agriculture.[24] Based on the model of the manual labor school, Oneida and schools like it had working farms attached to them where students could not only support themselves financially but also apply what they were learning. In effect, the farm was the student's laboratory, as well as a productive source of food for school and community. These schools flourished until the establishment of the land-grant colleges under the Morrill Act.

Similar patterns of early demand for education and the slowness of the established colleges to respond can be seen in a number of the applied scientific, technical, and engineering fields and in the area of business and commercial education.[25] Demonstrated social and economic demand led to the creation of for-profit schools to teach these subjects, which the established colleges did not offer. This is often the case today as well, with the for-profits capturing the market demand for flexible delivery of education in such fields as telecommunications, computer programming, and applied technology.

Education for Marginalized People

As one traces the historical roots of private, for-profit education in America, it becomes clear that such institutions sometimes played a particularly important role in opening up education to women, people of color, Native Americans, and those with disabilities, especially blind and deaf people. "If there were educational correlates of freedom that

were central to the life of the young Republic, there were also education correlates of oppression," wrote Lawrence Cremin, on the denial
of educational opportunities for blacks and Native Americans.[26] Cremin
also documents the common beliefs among white Americans that blacks
could not be assimilated into society and should not be taught to read
and write.[27]

By providing access to education for marginalized people, the for-
profits of the nineteenth century demonstrated how the profit motive
could work for the social good as well as for economic return. The
prevailing attitude toward the education of women, for example, was
conservative, to say the very least, in colonial and early America. With
few exceptions, the public "town schools" did not admit women, and
only men were allowed to expand their studies beyond reading, writing, and arithmetic. The town schools, supported by public money, typically resisted change of any kind in admissions practices and curricula.
The private, for-profit schools made education at all levels of instruction available to women and were soon located in the larger population
centers of New York, Boston, and Philadelphia, offering day and evening
instruction for men and women "in any subject for which there was a
demand."[28] Many private evening schools, most of which were apparently run on a for-profit basis, significantly expanded the educational
opportunities available to women beyond the domestic arts, into such
areas as writing, mathematics, music, dance, languages, geography,
history, and even into the male-dominated trades of bookkeeping and
surveying.[29]

Similarly, from 1800 to 1860 African American slaves and free persons of color were denied any form of education in the public schools
and colleges. Even after the slave system was abolished, teaching African Americans to read and write was a punishable offense in the southern states. Yet, such instruction actually flourished in what were called
"clandestine schools," run by private masters, some of whom were se-
verely sanctioned for their efforts. Individual entrepreneurs operating
outside the educational establishment first opened rudimentary education and technical training to African American children and adults.
These facts are recounted by Booker T. Washington in his classic essay
"Education of the Negro," written in 1899, when he was principal of
the Tuskegee Institute in Alabama.[30]

Proprietary schools also provided education to Native Americans. After the American Revolution, the country turned its attention to rebuilding the republic, and the need to provide education for Native Americans was somewhat neglected, except by groups of Protestant missionaries. The reservation schools had not yet been established, so independent teachers, working with missionaries, set up basic education programs for Native American children. One of the best-known schools of this type was the Brainerd Mission, in Georgia, established in 1817 and named after the Presbyterian missionary David Brainerd.

The Brainerd Mission provided practical education in agriculture, commerce, and the domestic arts to Cherokee children and adults, with the specific intent of rapidly assimilating them into white society.[31] Instruction was in English, and every student was given a new English name to replace his or her Native American name. Financial support was provided through a combination of tribal funds (derived from federal-government payments to the tribes in exchange for their relocation to less desirable lands) and Christian churches.[32] Some years later, when the reservation boarding-school system was failing, private industrial-training schools were established in towns near the reservations. An example is the Haskell Institute, in Lawrence, Kansas, founded in 1884 with a capacity for 550 students and including 30 buildings, its own waterworks, and a 650-acre farm. The institute enrolled both men and women of Native American descent, and the curriculum included instruction in many technical fields, along with vocal and instrumental music.[33] This institution has survived to this day. Now known as the non-profit Haskell Indian Nations University, it enrolls 1,000 students from 140 tribes and 38 states.

Education for the blind and deaf began as the private initiative of Thomas Hopkins Gallaudet in 1817.* Gallaudet studied methods for teaching the blind and the deaf in Europe and had schools operating in New England, New York, and Pennsylvania by 1831, all on a for-profit basis. These schools were viewed with great skepticism by the educa-

---

*Thomas Hopkins Gallaudet was the father of Edward M. Gallaudet, who, along with Amos Kendall, founded the National Deaf Mute College in 1864. The college was incorporated as Gallaudet College in 1954 and was recently renamed Gallaudet University.

tional establishment, but they soon became so successful that the federal and state governments got behind the movement to create more schools like them.[34]

In each of these instances, the individual, entrepreneurial efforts of private masters and their schools played a key role in the evolution of the American system of education. "Established in the seventeenth century, and continuing, without interruption, to the present day," wrote educational historian Robert Seybolt of the for-profit schools in 1925, "they have played a prominent part in the solution of the problem of providing education for all classes."[35] This role is an important and largely unacknowledged part of the legacy of proprietary education in the United States.

From Colonial America to the Information Age

The continuing development of for-profit institutions from 1850 to the turn of the century, through World Wars I and II, and from 1950 to the 1980s has been the subject of previous studies.[36] During these years the for-profit schools continued to respond to social and economic needs that were unmet by traditional colleges and universities. A number of the early for-profit institutions and their successors still survive today, such as Strayer University, founded in 1892 in Baltimore, and Rider University (now non-profit), founded in 1865 in Trenton, New Jersey, as one of the campuses of the Bryant and Stratton chain of for-profit business schools. For most of this time the for-profits were the invisible partners in the education industry, receiving little or no official recognition from federal or state governing bodies. As a result, there is no central source for records providing such basic data as the number of institutions and enrollments. Such information will have to be constructed from the surviving records of actual institutions, a task that falls outside the purpose of this book.

The New Higher-Education Industry

According to an article in the *National Review* in 1996, the new "education industry" was born as a news story in the *New York Times* in January 1996.[37] This pronouncement may or may not be accurate, but 1966 was certainly a banner year for for-profit higher education. The University of Phoenix, which in three years would become the nation's largest private university, became a publicly traded company in 1996. That was the year private investment capital began to flow into the business of education at a rate that caught the attention of Wall Street and the popular press. Leading investment houses, including Lehman Brothers and Salomon Smith Barney, held conferences to showcase thirty for-profit educational companies to potential investors. It was the year the Education Industry Group, a private industry watcher, developed and published the EI Index, which tracks 36 publicly traded education companies to provide a monthly barometer of stock performance for investors. It was also the year that the Integrated Postsecondary Education Data System (IPEDS), maintained by the National Center for Education Statistics, changed the definition of higher-education institutions to include private, for-profit schools eligible for federal financial-aid programs.[38]

Prior to 1996, the U.S. Department of Education had defined higher-education institutions as those that were *accredited as colleges* by an agency recognized by the secretary of education. This had the effect of excluding most for-profit institutions, which were not widely recognized as accredited *colleges,* even if they actually held regional association accreditation. The new criteria define higher-educational institutions in terms of eligibility for Title IV funding. To be eligible, institutions must offer an associate's degree or higher program consisting of at least 300 clock hours of instruction, possess accreditation recognized by the DOE, have been in business for at least two years, and have signed an agreement of participation with the DOE. This change made clear the criteria for recognition by the DOE, and in one year (1996) it increased the number of institutions included in the higher-education universe by 7.5 percent.

Under this new definition, the DOE now includes some 669 for-profit schools recognized as accredited colleges and universities. The most recent published statistics on the number of institutions include the following breakdown:

	Public Non Profit	*Private Non-Profit*	*Private For-Profit*
Four-year	615	1,536	169
Two-year	1,092	184	500

The 500 for-profit, two-year institutions operate as private community colleges offering a variety of associate's degrees and certificate programs. They are spread located in every state except Delaware, the District of Columbia, and Rhode Island. The largest concentrations are in Pennsylvania (72), California (51), Ohio (45), Florida (36), and New York (32). The 169 for-profit, four-year institutions represent an array of colleges and universities, including a few traditional liberal arts colleges that were acquired by educational corporations. Most of the four-year schools, however, specialize in business and technology fields. The largest concentrations by state include California (36), Florida (19), Colorado (12), and Illinois (11), while several states have none.

As noted in chapter 1, the actual number of for-profit colleges and universities operating in the United States is probably somewhat underrepresented in the IPEDS database. IPEDS depends upon information volunteered by institutions through surveys, and it is possible, even likely, that the number of for-profit schools is larger than currently reported by IPEDS. Until recently the federal government has only sporadically reported information on for-profit schools. A number of these institutions were either not polled or stopped sending in the information. For the academic year 2000–2001 the number of for-profit two- and four-year campuses in the United States is probably about 750.

The recent inclusion of for-profit institutions in the IPEDS database meant not only that the for-profits gained a measure of legitimacy as institutions of higher education but also that they would now be included in data gathered and reported by the NCES. In 1998–99 the category "private for-profit" appeared regularly in reports issued by NCES and in annual industry surveys, such as the almanac issue published by the *Chronicle of Higher Education*.

Adding the category "private for-profit" increased the total number of higher-education institutions recognized by the DOE to 4,096 in 1996. But literally thousands of for-profit postsecondary schools are still excluded from these numbers because they lack regional association accreditation.

The proprietary-school landscape in the United States is now huge. Approximately 7,000 such schools offer instruction beyond the secondary level in such fields as commercial art, electronics, food services and culinary arts, interior design, medical services, photography, and transportation. In terms of numbers of postsecondary schools, the for-profit sector is, and probably always has been, at least as large as the nonprofit sector. In recent years, however, it has become more visible, and as noted in chapter 1, it is the only segment of the higher-education industry that continues to grow.

Growth of the For-Profits

In 1991 there was only one for-profit postsecondary, degree-granting, accredited institution listed on the stock exchanges—DeVry, Inc., which became a public company that year. Eight years later, however, there were 40, of which 16 were "major players," according to industry analysts.[39] New initial and secondary public offerings are expected over the next several years as the new higher-education industry continues to grow and develop, and then probably taper off, with the strongest companies dominating the market. In the five years between 1994 and 1999 more than $4.8 billion in private investment capital was raised, through more than 30 initial public offerings and 30 follow-on offerings, to support new entries into the for-profit education market.[40] An estimated $500 million was raised in 1999 alone.[41]

In addition to the five publicly traded companies profiled in chapter 2, other companies are active in this segment of higher education. Quest Education Corporation (also mentioned in chapter 1) specializes in acquiring colleges. Quest operates 30 campuses in 11 states, all but one of which was purchased through acquisition. Many of the colleges the company buys are in financial trouble. The average age of these colleges at the time of acquisition is 35 years, although some were established a century ago. Part of Quest's strategy is not to change the names of the colleges it acquires, so that whatever value the name has in its market will be protected. "We don't change the names," says Gary Gerber, Quest's chairman and CEO, "because there is a franchise value in their communities."[42] Quest's strategy for continued growth and profitability is to identify colleges that are targets for acquisition and then integrate them into its existing system. "We believe that the fragmentation of the postsecondary education market provides significant opportunities to consolidate existing independently owned schools," say Quest's leaders. "We expect to utilize cash on hand, our bank credit facility, our common stock, and seller financing in connection with such acquisitions."[43] Quest is pursuing this strategy aggressively. In 1998 alone, the company acquired 12 campuses, including Hesser College in New Hampshire, Hamilton College in Iowa, and CHI Institute in Pennsylvania.

Another aggressive acquirer of existing schools is Corinthian Colleges, Inc., headquartered in Santa Ana, California. Corinthian currently operates 43 campuses in 17 states, divided into two major business groups: Corinthian Schools, Inc., which has a programmatic focus on diploma-level programs in allied health, and Rhodes Colleges, Inc., which focuses on associate's- and bachelor's-degree programs in business, information technology, and criminal justice. The company acquired the three campuses of Georgia Medical Institute in April 2000, adding to the Corinthian Schools side of the business what CEO David Moore describes as "the premier providers of training for entry-level allied health jobs in the Atlanta area."[44]

For-profit higher education as a sector also reaches well beyond the postsecondary level and includes many other private companies participating in various aspects of the privatization of the education industry as a whole. These other companies include educational management organizations (EMOs), which run elementary schools and preschools, such as Bright Horizons Family Solutions and Nobel Learning Centers; education service organizations (ESOs), such as Berlitz International and Sylvan Learning Systems; training and development providers, such as Caliber Learning Network and ITC Learning Corporation; at-risk-youth management companies, which run juvenile institutions and detention centers, such as ResCare and Ramsay Youth Services; and providers of educational products (software and learning tools), such as American Educational Products and Scholastic. Industry analysts use these categories of providers to develop indexes to track the education industry's performance.[45] There were more than 70 publicly traded companies in the education business in 1999, and the number has been growing quarterly.

As large and diverse as it is, the for-profit sector is still a relatively small part of the total education industry, representing approximately 10 percent, or $70 billion, of the total $750 billion spent annually in the

United States. Education is the second largest industry in the United States (behind health care), receiving twice the annual investments that national defense receives. Of the $750 billion spent annually, 75 percent is publicly funded and controlled by what might be called the educational establishment, which industry analysts refer to as a bureaucratic monopoly. Through new private initiatives and investment, however, higher education is in the early stages of diversification beyond the confines of a bureaucratic monopoly. The higher-education industry is now poised with potential, say some observers, for almost limitless growth. The combination of public and corporate dissatisfaction with traditional education, favorable demographic trends, and the infusion of a new kind of endowment—private investment capital— into the for-profit segment suggests that the for-profits will probably continue to take an increasing share of the education market.

Taking all these factors into consideration, it is not unreasonable to expect that the for-profits will continue to grow over the next decade until they represent approximately 25 percent of the postsecondary market in terms of total dollars spent annually.[46] Says Michael Heise, director of the Center for Education Law and Policy at Indiana University: "Investors are chiseling away at the dam of the last remaining government monopoly in the world. Were the dam to break, I expect there would be a flood of investment in educational research and development."[47]

The lines of demarcation between for-profit and non-profit also will continue to blur. Today, some of the for-profits have established non-profit foundations in order to receive gifts and grants. At the same time, the non-profits are continuing to launch their own for-profit ventures, such as New York University's for-profit School for Continuing Studies, National Technological University's for-profit venture-capital division, NTU Corporation, and Columbia University's digital-media division, called Morningside Ventures. Traditional universities and corporations are expected to continue to develop new and complex affiliations, suggesting to some observers that the difference between for-profit and non-profit higher education will eventually become so indistinct as to be largely meaningless to all but tax accountants.[48] (This blurring of the lines between for-profit and non-profit is explored further in chapter 6.)

The Simple Business of Education

Those of us who live and work inside academia (and I include myself here, even though I jumped ship to the for-profit sector) tend to think of higher education as a highly complex business. "It's not like making widgets," a former colleague liked to say whenever conversation turned to the bottom line during deans'-council meetings. Of course none of us had actually ever made widgets, but we were nonetheless quite confident that higher education was considerably more complex.

We insiders tend to regard the higher-education industry as an extremely complicated, multilayered network of regulations, institutional missions, governance processes, and traditions. We think of our institutions as complex entities, with confusing organizational structures, funded through elaborate and somewhat esoteric financial and budgeting processes, and serving myriad stakeholders, all with different needs and expectations. Higher education, we believe, is anything but simple and certainly much more complex than, say, manufacturing or banking or even the pharmaceutical industry. "Many in the academy," observes James Duderstadt, president emeritus of the University of Michigan, "would view with derision, or at least alarm, the depiction of the higher education enterprise as an industry, operating in a highly competitive, increasingly deregulated global marketplace."[49]

Higher-education industry analysts, who are outside experts looking in, have a different view of the business of higher education. Such analysts, trained as financial managers, market economists, and industrial sociologists, are not educators. They work for such organizations as Lehman Brothers, Salomon Smith Barney, and Merrill Lynch. Their job is to attract private investment capital to the publicly traded, for-profit providers and to monitor and predict the stock performance in these companies. In order to do that, they need to become skilled in assessing the big picture, watching and interpreting emerging trends, and reducing the economic realities of education to the language and symbolism of business. Many analysts with experience in other industries have moved into the higher-education sector in the past five years, and it is interesting that some of them, perhaps most, view higher education not as a highly complex business but as a simple one.[50]

For example, one such industry analyst asserts that the business of higher education is governed by only three essential financial metrics:

(1) enrollment, (2) the cost of acquiring customers, and (3) customer retention.[51] If an institution can lower the cost of acquiring its customers while maintaining enrollment and improving retention, it will generate increased revenue, favorable cash flow, and improved financial returns.

Analysts see higher education as having distinct business advantages over many other industries, especially since in their view higher education's products are not so much sold as bought. The distinction being made here between selling and buying is based on the difference between a market that must be created and one that creates itself. Higher education has value that is literally built into social and economic life in America. Student customers do not have to be sold on higher education; they already seek it out, in part because they know they can expect to gain an excess return on their educational investment, financially, socially, and in terms of career advancement.[52] In addition, because most of higher education's customers are retained for several years, revenue streams are predictable and the underlying fundamentals of the business are relatively stable.[53] The same cannot be said for many other businesses in many other industries.

The business of higher education probably is not as simple as some analysts suggest. But neither, perhaps, is it as complex as those on the inside would like to believe. The operation of a university is divisible by a complexity of units—colleges, schools, departments, disciplines, subdisciplines, and hundreds of individual courses—and structurally universities are indeed complex organizations. But we must differentiate between what universities do and how they go about doing it, on the one hand, and the essential business dynamics of an educational enterprise, on the other. Certainly, teaching, learning, the advancement of knowledge, and the formation of persons are complex processes. The governance structures and policies of universities are highly complex. Curricula are often complex. But the essential business dynamics of education, from the perspective of outside business experts looking in, are perceived to be relatively simple compared with those of other industries.

Still, the proposition that higher education is a simple business is not an easy one for those who live and work inside traditional academia to accept. So much energy and rhetoric have gone into convincing ourselves and others that we are highly complex, and that what we do is simply not translatable into the more mundane world of business and applied economics, that it is almost unthinkable to conclude that the education business is simple after all.

My goal here is not to try to reverse this thinking but to assert that there are knowledgeable experts in the business and economics of higher education who have concluded that the education business is in essence a comparatively simple one. There is perhaps a lesson here about the tendency of insiders to overcomplicate the business of higher education. Each of the big for-profit providers is demonstrating the value of keeping it simple.

The major companies in the for-profit university sector—Apollo, Argosy, DeVry, Education Management, and Strayer, among others such as Quest Education, Whitman Education, ITT, and Career Education—embody this philosophy. They have distilled the business of higher education into its no-frills essence. In each case, they have taken a simple and straightforward approach to the business of education and applied tried-and-true business practices to meet the needs of a market niche. They are doing so with considerable success in terms of growing enrollments, improved retention, and impressive levels of graduate placement, not to mention high profitability and very good returns on invested capital, all while meeting accreditation standards established by the non-profit sector. They have aligned themselves with what market economists identify as the fastest growing part of the American economy, the "knowledge sector of the service industry."[54] Their position in and relationship to this market are major factors in their success.

Trusting the Marketplace

Not too many years ago, *marketing* was an unwelcome word in academia, one of those terms borrowed from the world of business that represented a kind of self-promotion antithetical to the culture of non-profit higher education. I recall a deans'-council meeting at a private college in which the provost suggested that we should think about how we market our programs. Visibly offended, the dean of the school of liberal arts and sciences said, "My God, man, we're not a factory here!" Others around the table felt that talking about marketing was not in itself a bad idea, and since I was the business dean, that certainly included me, along with the deans of education and continuing studies, but we dropped the subject, mainly because of the force of the offended dean's response. In the face of his passionate argument that an institution of higher learning must be kept distinct from a business organization we had no equally passionate retort. Sometime later, marketing strategies in fact became a major feature of this college's strategic plan. After initially using outside marketing consultants, the college today has a senior administrator with the word *marketing* in her job title.

Today, virtually every college and university is deeply engaged in marketing, including, but not limited to, advertising, from direct mail and billboards to cable television and the Internet. Most colleges and universities now see themselves as market-driven institutions.[55] Yet there remains a significant difference in the way marketing is treated in for-profit universities as compared with the non-profits. Both employ marketing strategies enthusiastically and embrace the language of business when it comes to promotion and advertising, but the for-profits, as businesses, are distinctive in their understanding of the marketplace and in the way they approach it. In essence, the for-profits trust the market.

Trusting the market means behaving as if the market will tell you what it needs. It means approaching the market as if it were a benign and powerful source of information about real social and economic needs. To trust the market means to operate from the belief that a free-market economy, when it is functioning properly, tends to be self-correcting. The market needs to be read and understood, but it does not need to be changed. It *is* change.

Trusting the market in this way appears to be a radical and foreign notion for most non-profit colleges and universities. Although they acknowledge the reality of the market and are willing to respond to it, they generally do not regard it as trustworthy. They seem to cling stubbornly to the view that students and employers, for example, are fairly unsophisticated when it comes to the subject of learning, easily fooled by unscrupulous institutions, and generally do not readily know what is best for them in terms of education, degrees, fields of study, and so forth. Such a view has the potential of preventing institutions from treating students as intelligent customers. Employers too, because they often seem to want to hire only those graduates who have practical training

rather than those who are well rounded and truly learned, are sometimes regarded as if they themselves have to be reeducated. Indeed,
many non-profit universities often seem to behave as if part of their
responsibility is to educate, influence, and change the market in some
way. The advent of for-profit organizations embedded in non-profit institutions may be a signal that these attitudes are changing. The recent
innovative for-profit ventures at such institutions as Stanford, Columbia, Cornell, Maryland, New York University, National Technological
University, and Temple may mean that some non-profits will begin to
trust the market as traditional non-profit and for-profit boundaries begin to collapse.

Still, there is deep resistance within the academy to the notion of
for-profit ventures. When the venerable College Board announced in
1999 that it was launching a for-profit subsidiary to compete with online
test-preparation companies, some critics were appalled. "It's like put-
ting a Coke sign in a church," said Scott Rice, an English professor who
is writing a book on the influence of money on education.[56] In the end,
of course, non-profit universities will not change the market; the market will change them. "The only thing big enough and mean enough to
change professional behavior is the market," says Edward O'Neil, executive director of the Pew Health Professions Commission.[57]

The "market" in this case, as I have been suggesting, comprises two
primary demand streams: the interests of students and the needs of
employers. Students seek out certain kinds of academic programs, and
employers look for graduates with certain kinds of educational preparation. The for-profits strategically position themselves between these
two sets of demands and attempt to meet them in ways that satisfy
both. All of the for-profit institution's resources—admissions, degree
programs, curricula, faculty, classroom and laboratory facilities, placement efforts—are aligned with these market demands. The payoff for
trusting and responding to the market in this way is enrollment growth
and sustained employer demand for graduates. Both are essential to
the success of the for-profit university as a business enterprise.

What strikes me as remarkable about this rather simple formula is
that it has been used so rarely within the traditional non-profit environment of the higher-education industry. Even in such market-driven
programs as engineering and business administration most universities

are notoriously slow to respond to market demands. In my home state of New Jersey, for example, the former Department of Higher Education launched a program called the Business and Humanities Project in the early 1980s in response to growth in enrollments in business administration programs that was so large as to be considered almost unhealthy. Several university presidents were brought together with corporate CEOs around the state for the purpose of promoting awareness of the value of a liberal arts education for a business career. The credo of the group was that a liberal arts education was the single best preparation for a career in business and management. The CEOs nodded in polite agreement, but their college recruiters persisted in hiring the business-school graduates to fill jobs in the areas of demand, such as accounting, business finance, management, marketing, and computer applications for business. Ultimately, the project's funding was discontinued, and the project came to an end.

Beyond New Jersey, many traditional liberal arts colleges across the country added programs in business and management during the late 1980s, ten years into the significant and sustained enrollment growth in these fields. By 1990 the national market was saturated with business programs; then enrollments in business schools leveled off before beginning to drop sharply. Student interest and employer demand was now shifting to computer information systems, and many colleges and universities found themselves saddled with relatively new business programs for which the market was declining instead of growing.

The attitude of the traditional non-profit colleges and universities toward the marketplace is no doubt changing, but the change is coming slowly. Some presidents, such as Scott Cowen at Tulane, are in fact urging institutions to embrace market dynamics and warning that "we must stop thinking that marketplace forces are inconsistent with our mission and values."[58]

For-profit institutions are already there. They do not resist the market or attempt to change it by persuading students or employers that they need something other than what they want. If the market is demanding programs in wireless telecommunications, for example, they respond by creating a program in wireless telecommunications rather than saying to the market, "What you really want is our program in electrical engineering." They attempt, not to change the market, but to understand it and respond in a way that effectively meets its demands. This is the fundamental strategy of these institutions in positioning themselves in the education marketplace.

The Essence of the For-Profit Strategy

From their inception in colonial times as small evening schools run by private masters to today's multicampus corporate universities run by professional managers, for-profit institutions have consistently oriented themselves to the needs of the marketplace. They focus on working in harmony with the free-market economy, which, as we have seen, can also result in doing social good, since social needs are often related to economic opportunities. This premise, that social good and economic opportunity are tied together, is perhaps behind the privatization movement that has swept into health care, moved increasingly into government, and now begun to make new and significant inroads into education.

Doing social good, it must be said, is not the primary objective of for-profit universities. Their primary objective is to be successful businesses. One of their business drivers is providing greater access to higher education, which is one of the points at which economic opportunity meets social good. For example, African American students have continued to sustain distinctively high enrollments in for-profit higher education. At the DeVry and Strayer campuses, 40 percent of the students enrolled in the fall 1999 semester were African American. The journal *Black Issues in Higher Education* has reported that of the top 100 institutions awarding degrees to people of color in 1998, proprietary colleges were major providers. The top producer of minority baccalaureates in engineering-related technologies is a for-profit institution (ITT Technical Institutes), as are the number two and three producers of baccalaureates in computer and information science (Strayer and DeVry).[59]

Many factors account for the high minority enrollments in for-profit schools, including the location of the schools in population centers, fewer barriers to admission, high placement rates, and the availability of the full spectrum of financial aid. These are the kinds of factors mentioned by students themselves in several focus groups I conducted among DeVry students between 1997 and 1999. However, I would propose that it is also the case that because proprietary schools are themselves marginalized by the higher-education establishment, students who are marginalized by society may be drawn to them. Indeed, research into the social and psychological dynamics of student success as they relate to race and culture appears to provide support for this assertion.

Claude Steele's work, for example, suggests that many black students experience a stigma associated with academic performance and that this accounts for the underachievement of many blacks in academia.[60] Student focus groups at DeVry confirm this assertion. "When I go home, a lot of my friends resent me for being in school," said one student. "They think school is going to change me. I think that when reaching a goal, you sometimes have to leave people behind." Another student, from Ghana, said, "It is generally known in my culture that the people who leave to go to school are no longer in line with the culture. They are not around to learn from their parents and community. The family worries they will lose you."[61]

Steele and others have argued that black students do not identify with traditional education because to do so requires them to violate their own cultural identities, especially when they are the first in their families to attend college. To do well in school may be rewarding in some ways, but it also causes the anxiety of separation.[62] My own speculation is that going to a college like DeVry, ITT, Strayer, or some other for-profit institution may make it easier for black students to deal with this stigma since these schools are generally perceived as not representing traditional higher education.

For-profit universities do not have as their primary mission the shaping of a more informed citizenry, or creating a more cultured population, or helping young people understand their heritage, their society, and its values. Of course these things can and do happen in the natural course of a college education, even in the for-profits. When a dedicated and skilled teacher works with students who are capable and motivated, it does not matter whether the larger institution operates on a for-profit or a non-profit basis. When the social good is served, whether it is access to education by marginalized people or technical education in fields where there is a shortage of talent, it does not matter whether the holding company is tax-exempt or tax-paying.

4

The Financing of For-Profit
Higher Education

How the For-Profits Make Profits

Understanding the financing of for-profit universities and how their financial structures and processes differ from those of the non-profit sector requires answering some basic questions: How is income generated in these institutions? What are the sources of revenue? How is the money spent? What, exactly, is profit?[1]

On the surface, it is difficult to understand how educational institutions organized on a for-profit, tax-paying basis can generate substantial and sustained profits, while educational institutions organized on a non-profit, tax-subsidized basis often struggle just to break even. Not only do the for-profits pay taxes but they do not receive any donated funds from foundations, private donors, or federal, state, or local governments. Ninety percent of their revenue comes from tuition. How is it that a for-profit university charging $8,000 a year for tuition and fees can realize a gross profit margin of 40 percent, while a non-profit university may charge $25,000 for tuition and fees and just break even, or not even meet expenses, particularly when both institutions meet the same basic regional association accreditation standards? How do the for-profits do it?

To understand how the for-profits achieve profitability, imagine a regionally accredited university with a tightly focused mission of preparing students for the world of work. Imagine that this institution offers undergraduate and graduate degree programs only in fields for which there is a high marketplace demand. In fields for which there is little or no market demand, by either students or employers, degree programs are not offered. Imagine also that this university runs year round, fully utilizing its facilities during the day, evening, and weekends throughout the whole year. The full-time faculty do not have tenure, and 90 percent of them are fully deployed to teach. The energy of this institution and of almost all its employees is focused primarily on the success and satisfaction of its students.

Figure 4.1 identifies these and other characteristics typical of successful for-profit higher-education institutions, each of which is discussed below. Collectively, they are the ingredients for profitability.

Customer-Service Orientation

In his book *Managing Higher Education as a Business,* Robert Lenington, former chief financial officer at Bentley College, asserts that sooner rather than later higher education "will learn that the customer is king."[2] Lenington is referring to the reluctance, at least historically, of non-profit higher-education institutions to regard students as customers and their fear that the process of learning will be somehow damaged if they do so.

It must be said that the faculty in particular have often resisted the idea of responding to students as customers, perhaps fearing the loss of traditional authority, as well as the growing demand for greater accountability in their work as teachers. Peter Ewell, who counsels groups of faculty members on this issue in his work at the National Center for Higher Education Management Systems, says that when he suggests that students should be responded to as customers, it never fails to raise "an initial howl of protest."[3]

The growth in market share of for-profit colleges and universities during the 1990s has brought increased attention to the question

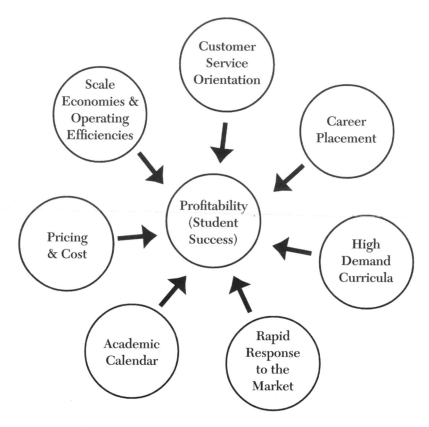

Fig. 4.1   The Ingredients of Profitability

whether it is appropriate and beneficial for higher-education institutions to treat students as customers. The for-profits, particularly the leading companies profiled in this book—Apollo, DeVry, Education Management, Argosy, and Strayer—devote considerable time and resources to understanding who their customers are and how to meet their needs, interests, and demands. They do this through a combination of market research, typically conducted by the corporate headquarters offices, industry advisory boards and student focus groups at the local campuses, and customer-relations training for staff employees who deal directly with students. These companies tend not to employ typical academic-department secretaries and opt instead for professional receptionists and customer-relations specialists.

In any service industry, the development of a strong customer-service orientation begins by clearly defining who the customer is. Many traditional academic institutions struggle with this seemingly simple first step. One private university where I was an academic dean engaged a consultant to help the institution adopt the principles of total quality management (TQM). As a first step, the consultant asked several groups of administrators and faculty to work in teams to answer the question, "Who is our customer?" This question kicked off a campus debate that lasted for several months. Relatively few members of the faculty seemed to feel that students were our primary customers. Some found the word *customer* offensive. The provost came out with a white paper on the subject that said that basically everyone was our customer. Two of the deans said that the faculty were their main customers, and it was suggested that the president considered the trustees his primary customers. In the end, it was decided at a meeting of the president's council that the principles of TQM did not apply to an institution of higher education. The consultant was fired.

Lack of clarity about who is the customer continues to be a fundamental challenge for many colleges and universities. In any business, especially in the service industries, says Daniel Julius, director of the Center for Strategic Leadership at the University of San Francisco, "not knowing who your customer is is probably fatal."[4] Most educational institutions readily acknowledge that they serve many different stakeholders—students, families, faculty, donors, alumni, trustees, employers, local communities, the general public—but they often seem to confuse stakeholders with customers.

In contrast, the for-profits do not struggle with the question of who the customer is. The customer is the student, and everyone—from the faculty to the librarians to the financial-aid office to the students themselves—is clear about it. Other important constituents and stakeholders, such as employers of graduates and investors in the business, are not considered customers.

Equally important, there is little confusion about what it means to effectively serve and satisfy this customer. The successful for-profit institutions—by which I mean those that balance growth, as evidenced by increasing enrollment, with academic quality, as evidenced by meeting regional and professional accreditation standards—have developed the capability to serve and satisfy their student customers without doing undue damage to academic integrity. Those who deal directly with students, such as the faculty, academic deans, librarians, registrar officers, and financial-aid staff, understand that satisfying the student customer does not mean, for example, giving away grades or giving in to every student demand. Good students, especially adult students with jobs and families, often demand rigor, and they know educational quality when they see it. I have talked with many adult students who were put off by instruction or a curriculum they perceived to lack sufficient depth and substance. Especially in the for-profits, where education is openly regarded as a consumable product and students are openly acknowledged to be the paying customers, the students are demanding consumers who expect a quality educational experience in exchange for their time and money. Serving the student customer, however, does not mean giving in to their every preference. To do so would be to lessen students' respect for the institution.

Serving the student customer is essentially a matter of being responsive. In a teaching and learning environment this involves listening to students' concerns, answering their questions, addressing their problems promptly and courteously, and explaining to them the rules (including giving a clear "no" when that is the appropriate response). Some non-profit institutions and faculty do all of this well, but others do not, especially, I believe, those that are unclear about whether students are indeed customers.

Whether or not we refer to them as customers, today's students are increasingly demanding consumers throughout all of higher education. Some campuses, in attempting to adopt the notion that students are customers, have found their efforts marred by what has been called "virtual adoption," a shift in language without a change in substance.[5] Virtual adoption is a kind of coping mechanism that some institutions have learned to use in the face of growing external demands for change. It has allowed some institutions to proclaim that they have adopted a customer-service orientation without changing the way they do business, or more accurately, without addressing the deeper issues within the culture of the institution that stand in the way of establishing a genuine customer-service orientation. "In the face of external pressure," writes Peter Ewell, "virtual adoption is a legitimate and valuable survival tool in a world that increasingly wants colleges and universities to engage in visibly businesslike practices."[6] The inadequacies of this technique are obvious. In the meantime, many of the for-profit competitors are providing real customer service to students, and the students are responding positively to this approach.

There was a time when going to college was regarded as a privilege. Fifty years ago students were expected to exhibit gratitude and humility for the opportunity to study with professors, and many of them did. Today, however, going to college is viewed by many students as a right and a consumable good.

Recently I met with a student who was complaining about the amount of work required of him in several of his classes at DeVry. He had been consistently unsatisfied with the responses he received about this concern from his professors, the department chair, and the dean, so he came to me. I listened to his complaints about the amount of reading he was assigned, frequent quizzes in one course, and three papers that were required for another. After he had said his piece, I shifted the conversation to his sense of responsibility for his own learning. He had little appreciation for this line of argument. His view was that he had paid his tuition and now he should be taught. He had no real sense of his own responsibility in the matter of his learning beyond that of paying the tuition, buying books, and showing up for class.

I suspect that many faculty, deans, and advisers in every kind of educational institution could tell similar stories. Nonetheless, being customer oriented with today's students basically requires that an institution respond to the mindset of this kind of student. The for-profits, in my experience, tend to accept this reality much more easily than do many non-profit institutions. In the for-profit environment the success of the students is the top priority for faculty, administrators, and support staff. They know that the customer is king.

In these institutions, student success is interpreted to mean both academic success, as measured by successful progression through and completion of a program of study, and career launching upon graduation, as measured by placement in a job related to the program of study at a good salary, preferably one that offers opportunity for career advancement. The more traditional, abstract notion of learning for its own sake and the idea of cultivating knowledge that appears to lack utilitarian value do not resonate with a growing number of today's students and their families. The ideas of program completion and job placement, however, stand on common ground with students and the institution. When students are successful, they get what they came for, and the institution is assured continued growth, ongoing market demand, and profitability.

Learning, it must be acknowledged, can still occur in this kind of environment. As I noted earlier, whenever good teaching and motivated students meet—even if it is seen by students as basically a means to an end—the higher goals of opening minds, expanding insight, and increasing knowledge can occur, or at least the potential is there.

Career Placement

Perhaps the ultimate outcomes measure in the for-profit university is the placement of graduates. In many ways, it is placement that drives the whole system, for placement (or, in some cases, career advancement) is both the goal of the student customer and the tangible indicator of the value of the degree in the marketplace.

The career-placement performance of the five largest for-profit providers is shown in table 4.2 (p. 103). The placement rates shown, ranging from 96 percent at DeVry to 79 percent at Strayer, indicate the proportion of graduating students placed in careers related to their educational program within six months of graduation. Comparable data from the non-profit sector are not available because non-profit institutions generally do not report placement rates, and some place a higher value on the percentage of undergraduates who go on to graduate school than on the percentage who get jobs following graduation. There is little question that for-profit placement rates are among the highest in the higher-education industry. Placement of graduates in jobs related to their education is both a key business metric and a prime indicator of how well a career-oriented institution is achieving its academic mission.

Career placement of graduates is viewed by industry analysts as a measure of the return on educational investment (ROEI) that students can expect after they graduate. One or two higher-education industry watchers have projected that the average ROEI for a U.S. bachelor's degree is 18.7 percent.[7] This calculation represents an estimate of the financial return a graduating student can expect, on average, after paying for his or her college education (including student loans) and entering the work force with a bachelor's degree. However, the ROEI for a bachelor's degree from a for-profit institution jumps to 28 percent because of the emphasis in these institutions on offering high-demand curricula. In computer-related fields, for example, the average starting salary for students with a bachelor's degree was more than $42,000 in 1998. In the high-technology computer-related fields the ROEI is projected to increase to more than 35 percent by 2002.[8]

The for-profits intentionally position themselves in fields of education that will yield successful placement and a high ROEI. As long as employers seek graduates, there will be enrollment demand for programs. Both are necessary for sustained profitability.

High-Demand Curricula

For-profit universities orient their curricula to specific needs of the marketplace. They only offer academic programs for which there is a strong, unmet occupational demand and for which a strong future demand is evident. The list of for-profit degree programs correlates closely with the list of career openings appearing in most large metropolitan newspapers. During the mid-1990s, for example, the Sunday edition of the *New York Times* listed hundreds of positions each week in information technology, telecommunications, network administration, and computer information systems. Entry into one of these fields almost always requires a college degree in that field. Several of the largest for-profits have aligned themselves with this demand. As business enterprises, they have excelled at finding out what kinds of academic preparation employers want, then translating that need into a curriculum that emphasizes the application of knowledge and the development of skills.

As related in chapter 3, this approach of identifying unmet needs in the market and then designing programs to meet those needs appeals to the two main aspects of the marketplace served by the for-profit university—students and employers. An important distinction between how the typical for-profit institution and the typical non-profit institution approach these market forces is that the for-profits do not try to define for these forces what they need educationally so much as respond to what they express as their needs. The emphasis is not on telling the market what it needs but on continuously gathering information from the market and then responding. The for-profit providers do this by carefully monitoring changes in the data at hand, such as student interest in program offerings (measured by inquiries, applications, and enrollment shifts) and employer demand (measured by requests to interview graduating students, job offers, and placement rates for each program). They also track industry trends reported by analysts, looking for emerging opportunities for new programs. Some of the for-profit providers hire consultants who specialize in emerging industries, much in the same way that some universities hire lobbyists to follow their interests in state capitals and in Washington.

Reading the marketplace is not a particularly complex or sophisticated process. It basically involves paying attention to data readily available to the institution at its front door in the form of admissions and enrollment trends, and at its back door in the form of trends in the placement of graduates. Having lived and worked in both non-profit and for-profit universities, I think the essential difference is that the for-profits pay far more attention to this information, just as any successful business in any industry would do.

In responding to the market, the for-profits do not attempt, as do many non-profit colleges, to establish a market niche simply on the basis of academic programs that are unique among competitors. The emphasis is on finding a response that is effective, not on offering educational products that cannot be found elsewhere, a strategy that non-profit institutions might do well to follow.

The *Chronicle of Higher Education* recently described the plight of a group of small, relatively unknown liberal arts colleges that are struggling to survive.[9] These are institutions with fewer than 750 students, located in small towns across America, that cannot attract many students from outside their own regions. Even during the economic boom of the 1990s such institutions closed their doors at a rate of about two a year, according to data collected by the DOE. The financial problem facing these institutions can really only be solved through enrollment increases. In search of students, some of them have mistakenly decided that the key to attracting students is program uniqueness. The danger in this approach is choosing programs that are so unique as to lack sufficient market demand, as in the case of the small midwestern college described in the *Chronicle* article.

In higher education, market demand probably has more impact on profitability than does market uniqueness. Demand plus uniqueness is a strong combination, but demand is essential. If the programs of for-profit institutions appear to be unique, it is because these organizations are more closely attuned to the needs of the market than are many non-profit schools. For example, DeVry's campus in New Jersey began offering a new bachelor's degree program in telecommunications management in 2000. This was the first degree in this field offered at the baccalaureate level in New Jersey, even though the state is home to a large concentration of employers in the telecommunications industry.

By offering programs that are in high demand and not offering programs that are not, the for-profits focus their resources in ways that can sustain growth and high volume, both of which are essential to realizing the scale economies needed to run a profitable enterprise. By positioning themselves in the marketplace to ensure continuing demand by students and by employers of graduates, they ensure strong and predictable revenue streams.

Rapid Response to the Market

After twenty years as an administrator in non-profit institutions, both public and private, I could easily see that change happens remarkably quickly in the for-profits, especially when it comes to the curriculum. Changes in course content, as well as the addition and deletion of some courses, typically occur every semester in the for-profit institutions in response to input from students, employers, accreditation requirements, improvements in pedagogy, and changes in technology. New degree programs are introduced as often as two or three times in a single year in these institutions. Programs for which demand no longer exists are discontinued, which is something I think I never saw during all my years in non-profit institutions. With the added benefits of coordinating resources of a home office and multiple campus sites where programs can be piloted and then replicated at other locations, the energy of the institution is geared toward continual change.

Whole new programs sometimes go from development to launch within a matter of months in for-profit universities. A good example is DeVry's certificate program in information technology (IT). The program requires an earned bachelor's degree for admission. In just three semesters it provides students with the basic technical core courses for a degree in IT. It is designed primarily for students who want to enter the booming IT field but have a degree in some other discipline. Piloted at one of the Toronto campuses in 1998, the program was introduced in the United States at the Phoenix, Arizona, campus a few months later. Students and employers responded enthusiastically. By the end of 1999 the IT program had been "rolled out" (to use DeVry parlance, familiar in the automobile industry) at several other DeVry campuses in the United States, using the Toronto and Arizona curricula as models.

Faculty are always involved in these change processes, but they do not have the final authority to approve curriculum changes. These decisions are made by the business side of the organization. Traditional educators may find this arrangement inappropriate, but the for-profits tend to regard the faculty as experts in teaching and delivery, not necessarily in creating a curriculum or developing a new degree program in response to the market. Thus, a distinction is made here between subject-matter expertise and curriculum expertise. Development of new programs is a team effort involving people from marketing, admissions, financial aid, and placement, as well as the academic side. Academic debates concerning issues of discipline content and program ownership still occur, but they are short lived. It is surprising to me how nimble an educational institution can be in such an environment.

Debates over the curriculum regularly take years in non-profit institutions and sometimes result in no change whatsoever. At one college where I served on the core-curriculum committee, the committee actually met continuously for ten years, often rehashing the same ground. One member of the committee died before the committee made its final recommendation. In the end, the committee recommended no changes in the college's core curriculum.

Non-profit higher education has always been somewhat market-driven, but by business standards it has not been very market-responsive. In essence, this lack of market-responsiveness probably stems from the slow and cumbersome decision-making process that has long characterized higher education. While the intent has perhaps been to make better decisions rather than quick ones, in my view, this has been somewhat of an illusion. The outcome of what might be termed excessive and prolonged participation in decision making has sometimes been no decision at all. Daniel Julius, J. V. Baldridge, and J. Pfeffer argue that decision making in traditional higher education is actually a delusion. "Decisions are not really made," they write; "instead, they come unstuck, are reversed, get unmade during the execution, or lose their impact as powerful political groups fight them."[10] The point is that to respond to the market requires making good decisions, often quickly. The effectiveness of decisions made by the for-profits is based not on taking the time to process everybody's input or on reaching consensus but on how well the decision responds to the marketplace.

Academic Calendar

The academic calendar in the for-profits is governed by two objectives: optimal use of facilities and customer convenience. Classes run year round, so that is possible for students to complete a four-year bachelor's degree in three years. Consequently, there is no time during the summer months when facilities are underutilized. Class schedules are organized in clusters during the day, the evening, and the weekend to allow students to maintain full- or part-time jobs while attending school full time. It is often possible for full-time day students to have either morning or afternoon schedules. Commencements are typically held three times a year, so there is a steady stream of graduates completing programs and entering the job market. In contrast to the academic calendar of the non-profit university, that of the for-profits is not based on either tradition or faculty convenience.

Pricing and Cost

By *pricing* I mean the tuition level and the strategy used for setting it. By *cost* I mean how much it costs the institution to educate students and how those costs are controlled. One reason why the for-profits are profitable is that they intentionally set their tuition at a level that will allow them to make a profit to be made while remaining competitive and financially accessible to their student market. In setting tuition levels, they consider both what the market will bear and what the competition charges. Almost all the for-profits set their tuition somewhere between those charged by public and private non-profit institutions.

Conversely, the pricing strategy of many non-profit universities grows out of how much revenue is needed in order to create a balanced budget and to afford the kind of campus facilities and programs desired by the faculty, students, and staff.

Over the past twenty years the price of an undergraduate education in real dollars has doubled, and during the decade of the 1990s average tuition prices increased at more than twice the rate of the average U.S. household income.[11] Because the price of a college education has continued to increase faster than other economic indicators, many institutions may be on the verge of pricing themselves out of their markets.

When pressured to explain why tuition prices continue to rise more sharply than the rate of economic inflation, non-profit colleges and universities often say that tuition increases are necessary because their own costs keep rising. That claim is misleading, says Mathew Miller, a senior fellow at the Annenberg Public Policy Center. "Colleges, like all non-profits, raise all the money they can and then spend it."[12] Miller further suggests that much of the cost incurred by the non-profits is not directly relevant to the students' education. One reason for this is the increasing level of market competition among non-profit institutions, which has fueled the creation of costly amenities, especially those related to expenditures on the physical plant budgets, which may have little to do, directly, with the quality of education.[13] The for-profits, on the other hand, keep costly amenities to a minimum by offering a no-frills option, allocating resources instead to expenses that have a direct relationship to students' education, such as classroom facilities, instructional laboratories, and educational technology.

This distinction is evident in the budget-approval processes of the for-profits. When deans and faculty propose capital expenditures for classrooms and laboratory equipment, for example, they are normally approved without delay. This is a business decision rather than a political decision. When new computers are ordered to replace older equipment, for example, areas where student usage is high, such as the labs and library, receive them first. Requests for capital expenditures that are not obviously related to the students' educational experience, such as new furniture for administrative offices, require special approval and must be budgeted well in advance.

Costs are painstakingly measured and controlled in the for-profits, with the result that the average cost of educating a student is often much lower than in the non-profits. The average cost *to the institution* of educating an undergraduate student for two semesters at public and private non-profit and for-profit institutions are shown below:*

Public	*Private*	*For-Profit*
$17,026	$23,063	$6,940

From these figures it is evident why the for-profit providers are able to hold down the price of tuition: their costs are substantially lower. In contrast, many non-profit colleges and universities do not regularly measure and track their costs. Indeed, some still operate without any form of costing system.[14]

By holding down costs that are not perceived to be directly related to instruction and instructional support, the for-profits create the opportunity for profitability and are less dependent on price increases to cover costs. Consequently, tuition increases in the typical for-profit university averaged 3 percent to 4 percent annually during the 1990s. Similar efforts to eliminate programs and projects that are not directly related to instruction are beginning to take place in the non-profit sector. In the Massachusetts public university system, for example, the board of higher education has "urged the reduction of 'public service' projects that have little to do with students and teaching," with the goal of stabilizing rapidly increasing costs.[15]

By doing without expensive student residence halls, stadiums, faculty dining rooms, sports teams, and president's houses, and by minimizing faculty release time for nonteaching activities, the for-profits are able to keep the cost of educating a student at the same level as the price of tuition, or very close to it. The real business elegance of this strategy is that the for-profits have been able to stabilize the relationship between the cost of educating a student and the tuition charge, so that tuition actually covers the cost of the education provided. Then, by taking advantage of economies of scale, the for-profits are able to

*The figures shown represent combined educational and general budgeted expenditures per student for two semesters in 1997–98. The for-profit figure is for DeVry Institutes of Technology. The other averages were based on the National Center for Higher Education Statistics, Mini-Digest of Education Statistics, available at *http://nces.ed.gov/pubs98/MiniDigest97.*

leverage a profit by enrolling a sufficient volume of students in each academic program. Sufficient enrollment volume combined with enrollment growth results in stable costs and predictable revenues.

Scale Economies and Operating Efficiencies

Achieving economies of scale can lower costs and increase operating efficiencies in any organization. Studies have shown that in the University of California system, for example, as campus size increases, the proportion of the budget allocated to administrative expenses can be reduced. "Such an economy of scale," writes Frederick Balderston, a former faculty member at Berkeley and author of *Managing Today's University*, "could then be built into a declining-percentage budgetary standard for general administrative expense budgeting."[16]

As businesses accountable to stockholders, the for-profits place a high value on running their operations efficiently and taking advantage of economies of scale. For example, one of the obvious keys to maximizing efficiency is to control class sizes. The emphasis in the for-profits, however, is not on running large classes but on reducing and eliminating very small ones. On my DeVry campus, with 3,500 students, the average class size is 37, and the largest classes have 65 students. Classes in some areas of the curriculum, such as composition, are kept to an average of 27. Like almost all the for-profits, DeVry has found that classes in the range of 30 to 40 students seem to optimize learning, student retention, and efficient deployment of the faculty. However, great care is taken in designing and managing the class schedule to avoid small classes, say, below 15. This is accomplished by closely monitoring the enrollment and registration numbers right up to the start of classes each semester. Last-minute adjustments, such as collapsing two underenrolled sections of a course into one or adding a new section to a course that is overenrolled, are routine.

Now, one consequence of making these last-minute corrections to the class schedule is that some members of the faculty do not know what their final teaching schedule is until right before the semester begins. This inconvenience is outweighed by the need to serve the customer and manage the business, both of which are higher priorities than the convenience of the faculty. Most for-profit faculty understand

and accept this as one of the realities of working in an educational environment that responds to students as customers.

Controlling class size also allows the institution to maximize the efficient use of facilities. Classrooms in the typical for-profit are intentionally built and furnished to house classes of 35 to 50 students, with a few smaller seminar rooms and a few larger classrooms to handle the occasional large class of 70 to 80 students.

The size of the entering class in each academic program is also carefully monitored. At a minimum, at least 15 new students must enter each program each semester. Actually, the entering classes usually number several hundred, but should the number drop below 15, the classes will not be offered that semester. The admissions staff watch these numbers carefully, for they are the ones who have to inform the students if classes do not run. Not surprisingly, that rarely happens.

These eight factors in figure 4.1 are the ingredients for profitability in the for-profit sector. Any one of these alone probably would not be sufficient. Taken together, however, they provide a powerful combination of business and academic practices that result in profitability. Profit, of course, is a necessary outcome. I argue in the next section, however, that the necessity of profit is not limited to the for-profit institutions of higher education.

Profit: What Is It Really?

"To pursue profit is to pursue creation," says Mark Da Cunha, author of the website *www.capitalism.org*. Da Cunha argues that profit is the result, not of greed, but of creativity. In order to make a profit, you must first create something—an object, process, or idea—that others will find of value. "Your profit is the symbol and reward for the value of your creation," he asserts, "as judged by those who have freely given of their wealth to you in exchange for it."[17] Da Cunha suggests that the profit motive is inherently a good thing and that its opposite, the loss motive, is inherently a bad thing. Of course, we rarely hear about the loss motive since losses usually occur when organizations fail to achieve their goals. Losses can be anticipated and may even be planned for, but organizations rarely, if ever, are motivated to realize them. By their very nature, all healthy organizations are motivated to realize a return on their investments—a profit of some kind—whether they call themselves for-profit or non-profit.

The *Oxford English Dictionary* suggests that the word *profit* does indeed stand for something entirely positive. As a noun, *profit* is described by such words as *advance, progress, gain, good, benefit,* and *well-being,* and as a verb it is defined as *to make progress, advance, go forward, improve, prosper, grow.* Profit is an essential feature of a free-market economy. Profit is the monetary difference between the cost of providing a product or service and the price received for that product or service. In higher education, profit is the difference between the cost of providing an education and the revenue received in exchange for that service.

Non-profit educational institutions presumably do not make profits and do not operate according to the profit motive. In contrast, for-profit institutions presumably exist to make money and are governed by the profit motive. Such distinctions, however, appear to be more a matter of language than of actual financial practices, although, as we have seen, there are also some differences in financial practices.

Profit and "Excess Revenue"

It must be stated that many non-profit colleges and universities do, in fact, make profits. Indeed, they need to generate profits for capital formation, and access to capital is essential for institutional growth, maintenance of quality, and even survival. Robert Lenington argues that "in fact, most institutions do earn a profit and quietly shuffle it between funds. If they did not earn a profit and reinvest it in the business to develop, they would still be at the starting gate financially."[18] A small number of the non-profits, like Harvard University, generate profits in the hundreds of millions of dollars each year. Harvard takes in more than $150 million annually in excess revenue through continuing-education classes alone, about 10 percent of its $1.5 billion operating budget, and then allocates this profit to subsidize other programs within the university.[19]

Most institutions, however, enjoy more modest profits, ranging from several thousand to several hundred thousand dollars in a good year. The language used to describe this profit is "excess of revenues over expenditures and mandatory transfers." In other words, after all expenses are paid and required fund transfers are made at year-end, there is often money left over, called "excess revenue." To my thinking there is no substantive difference between excess revenue and profit. Both are the financial gain that remains after expenses are paid. Of course, no taxes are paid on excess revenue, since non-profit institutions are tax-exempt.

One further distinction sometimes made between excess revenue and profit is that non-profit organizations are required to operate under a "non-distribution constraint," which prohibits the distribution of profits directly to the owners. In contrast, the for-profits are called "proprietary" because they have owners to whom a share of the profits is distributed. In the case of the publicly traded education companies like Apollo and Argosy, among several others, the owners, primarily private individuals, are the stockholders. When these companies make profits, a portion is distributed to the stockholders in the form of equity or dividends, or both. Since non-profits do not have owners, at least in the sense of stockholders, they do not distribute their profits in this way.* Nonetheless, in practice many non-profit institutions deposit excess revenues in quasi endowment funds and then proceed to use the revenues for a number of purposes, including distribution, sometimes to the faculty in the form of salary increases.

Thus, the distinction between for-profit and non-profit in higher education apparently is not a matter of profit at all, for that distinction is essentially a difference of language and, perhaps, accounting practice. The truer distinction between for-profit and non-profit is a matter of taxation. The for-profits are tax-paying and the non-profits are tax-exempt. Because non-profits do not pay any taxes, they are bound by the non-distribution constraint, which requires that excess revenue over expenses be reinvested in the organization and not distributed to the owners. As noted earlier, Milton Friedman, the Pulitzer Prize–winning

---

*Although the non-profits do not have owners in the sense of stockholders, it may not be accurate to say that nobody owns them. My experience is that many groups act as if they own the non-profit university. The faculty, for example, often act as if they are the institution's owners. Trustees too sometimes seem to construe their fiduciary responsibility as a kind of ownership. In the case of public universities, the state itself and, by extension, the citizen taxpayers may consider themselves the owners of the institution.

economist, has argued for years that we should do away with the terms *non-profit* and *for-profit* in higher education, because these terms are both misleading and inaccurate. The meaningful difference, says Friedman, is between *tax-paying* and *tax-avoiding*.[20]

The Profit Motive and the Spending Motive

For-profit educational institutions unabashedly seek to realize an excess of revenues over expenditures, for this is part of their business reality and their responsibility to stockholders. Some people may find this profit motive antithetical to the mission of an educational institution. Yet, as I have argued, the profit motive is also alive and well in the non-profits. Like the for-profits, they are compelled to generate profits from current operations, and they consciously anticipate and plan for such "excess revenues" as part of the budgeting process.[21]

The case can be made that the for-profit university is actually a more forthright form of enterprise than is the non-profit university when it comes to finances. Publicly held companies operate with their books open to the public, and they must file detailed quarterly financial reports with the Securities and Exchange Commission. In these organizations there is no hidden profit motive, no lack of accountability for the use of financial resources, and no pretense about the profit motive. If there were no profits to be made in higher education, these companies would not have entered the industry in the first place.

Spending assumes a role that has particular meaning in the non-profits, one that is fundamental to the way unit managers support and protect their operations. Often masquerading as the desire to break even, the spending motive is the practice of spending all the money allocated to budgeted expenditures even if all of it is not needed. In the non-profits, funds are normally spent as originally budgeted for fear that otherwise they will disappear from the next year's budget allocation.

Academic administrators know what will happen if they do not spend the full amount of their budgets by the end of the fiscal year: they will have to turn back those funds. Consequently, at many non-profit institutions there is often a flurry of spending as the fiscal year draws to a close. Wise to this, some chief financial officers have instituted a spending freeze one or two months before the end of the fiscal year, which simply means that units have to spend their allocations earlier in the year rather than waiting until the end. It could be argued that managers in for-profit entities, especially in overhead and staffing areas, spend out their budgets in the same way. My own experience, however, is that the for-profits more closely monitor budget spending throughout the fiscal year, with the result that year-end spending is neither excessive nor a surprise.

All of this produces a huge "disincentive to economical management," to use Frederick Balderston's phrase. Ending the fiscal year with unspent balances can actually harm future budgets, which are typically built on the prior year's expense history. The net effect on the motivation to save money, says Balderston, is "chilling."[22] With little or no financial incentive to increase operating efficiency, and confronted with a significant disincentive to generate savings, administrators in the non-profits naturally fall prey to the spending motive.

This is one of the fundamental reasons why some organizations that were once organized on a non-profit basis—such as museums, art galleries, symphonies, and hospitals—are being reformed as for-profit entities. In the not too distant past such changes would have been unthinkable. Charles Kolb, general counsel for United Way of America and former deputy under secretary for planning, budget, and evaluation at the DOE, describes the spending motive as an inverse correlation between spending and performance.[23] He argues that the combination of excessive fraud and mismanagement have produced a new demand for accountability in non-profit organizations of every kind. It was perhaps only a matter of time before such changes would take root in higher education. Two of the lessons being learned in the process are that profitability is not inherently a bad thing and that the profit motive is not necessarily inconsistent with the social good.

Profit and the Social Good

For most of his career, Benno Schmidt Jr. was a believer in the non-profit model of education and a champion of some of its primary values, namely, freedom of expression and the value of a classical liberal arts education. As Yale's twentieth president, Schmidt was an outspoken voice for traditional higher education. A consummate fundraiser, he built Yale's endowment to a level where it had the highest growth rate of any private university, including Harvard.

Schmidt surprised many of his colleagues and friends when he left Yale in 1992 to become CEO of the Edison Project, an aggressive for-profit education company that today operates eighty elementary schools. "They thought I was crazy," he recalled at a recent conference in New York.[24] Having experienced a conversion of sorts, Schmidt has now become an outspoken advocate for the other side.

"It's pure myth that the market and profit are antithetical to serving society," he says. Schmidt has seen firsthand the extent to which profit-making companies infuse their financial resources as donated income to support the causes of freedom of expression and liberal learning. Schmidt says that since leaving the university and entering the world of profits he has been "shocked at the altruism of for-profit organizations."[25] This altruism is reflected in part by the extent to which private-sector companies invest money in America's social and economic future, primarily in the form of spending on research and development. Such investment has tangible results.

"Perhaps the most significant engine of economic growth in the U.S. over the past three decades," say market watchers at Merrill Lynch, "has been the new products and technologies made possible by research and development."[26] Microsoft, for example, spends 17 percent of its revenues on research and development, or $2.5 billion in 1998. Intel spends 10 percent on R&D; Merck, 7 percent; and General Motors put $7.9 billion in R&D, or 6 percent of its $140.4 billion in revenues, in 1998.*

Profits and the social good are not necessarily in opposition, and sometimes they work in harmony, as we saw in chapter 3 with regard to proprietary education's important role in the education of marginalized people. This point made, however, there remain some fundamental questions about the current and future place of for-profit higher education in achieving the higher purposes we have traditionally considered appropriate for higher education.

---

*In contrast, K–12 public education in the United States has annual revenues of more than $330 billion and spends less than 0.1 percent on R&D. Attempting to address this problem, the President's Committee of Advisors on Science and Technology recently called for "a quintupling of federal educational research to $1.5 billion," which would increase the amount spent on R&D to 0.5 percent of revenues.

Howard Gardner, in *The Disciplined Mind: What All Students Should Understand,* says that the essential content of a proper education boils down to three things: truth, beauty, and morality.[27] If it is true that the social good and the profit motive can work in harmony, is it also true that the for-profit college or university can provide an education that revolves around truth, beauty, and morality? Are the for-profits really providing an education to students, or are they merely in the business of providing credentials and job training for a fee? Should we ask the same questions of the non-profits?

These are important questions that arise naturally out of any serious discussion of the corporate profit motive and the mission of an educational institution. We will consider them more fully in the next two chapters. Before leaving the subject of the profit motive, however, we need to acknowledge its darker side, especially as it pertains to the business of providing a higher education.

The Darker Side of the Profit Motive—Greed and Sales

In my work in and study of for-profit colleges and universities I have observed a darker side of the profit motive that takes two different forms: greed and sales. Greed, in this context, is the unchecked desire for increasing profitability. This unchecked desire, in my view, is not so much a problem of individual companies or their leaders as it is a dominant force within the market-based economy itself. Stockholders demand a good return on their investments. Publicly held companies are dependent on profitability for their very existence. As a business enterprise with an academic mission, the for-profit university is sometimes caught between the strengths of its two, opposing personalities. One side seeks to satisfy the unquenchable desire for greater income, larger profit margins, and greater return to stockholders' equity. The other side's passion is teaching and learning, and the formation of educated persons. Often, as I argue throughout this book, the two coexist fairly peacefully, agreeing to disagree at points of impasse. In such moments the business side allows the academic side to do its thing, which it seems to seldom fully understand beyond a fairly superficial level, while the academic side concedes that the financial health of the institution provides a form of practical support that is necessary. At other times the tension between these two forces is not benign. At such times the academic side clearly takes a back seat, for the business side holds the ultimate trump card: without the business side, the academic side would cease to exist. In these moments the financial imperative—let's call it greed—threatens to obliterate Howard Gardner's triune educational virtues of truth, beauty, and morality.

For example, as I related in chapter 2, all of the for-profit institutions I have studied are reluctant to invest in libraries, which are viewed by the business side as pure expense. Apollo's libraries are entirely online, Strayer has several campuses, each with only a few thousand volumes, Education Management's libraries house only about 10,000 volumes, and even DeVry, which was required by the North Central Association to invest more in its libraries, remains reluctant to build most of its campus libraries beyond about 30,000 volumes. The reason is simple: however important libraries may be, they are expensive and unprofitable, they occupy what operations managers view as unproductive space, and therefore they reduce profit margins.

The other aspect of the darker side of the profit motive in higher education is the emphasis on sales. In the for-profits, the admissions offices are basically sales organizations, and the admissions staff is made up of salespeople. As such, they use selling techniques to enroll students, leading them through a decision process that, however inadvertently, is not always based on accurate information, may sometimes lead to a certain amount of misrepresentation, and usually involves sales closure tactics that pressure students to sign up.

Occasionally this sales pressure backfires. For example, Education Management Corporation, which operates the art institutes in major cities across the country, was sued in 1999 by 145 former and current students at its Art Institute of Houston. The students alleged that they were "misled about the benefits or quality of educational services provided to them."[28] Presumably, this "misleading" occurred at the front end, when they were given a sales pitch by the sales force. As of this writing, 90 additional litigants have joined the lawsuit, which has not yet been settled. Whether these students were actually misled is now a legal question to be decided by the courts. The point, however, is that many of them apparently felt they were misled.

In other cases, however, this kind of sales pressure is just what the prospective student may need. I have talked with graduates who, looking back, were grateful for the extra "push" that got them in the door and into a new career. But the emphasis on selling may rob some students of sufficient time for careful reflection about choice of a major and career options. Every semester at some of the for-profits a certain percentage of new students are enrolled who probably have no business being there. While the same can be said of many non-profit colleges and universities, the difference in the for-profits is that someone explicitly sold them.

Having acknowledged these two aspects of the darker side, let us now look at where the money comes from and where it goes in the for-profit institution.

Sources of Revenue

Table 4.1 compares sources of revenue for public and private non-profit and for-profit institutions of higher education. Not surprisingly, the largest single source of revenue for non-profit public colleges and universities is subsidies from state governments, at 35.9 percent of total revenues. Adding in federal and local government subsidies brings the total to 51 percent. This financial support comes directly from the citizenry in the form of taxes.

Private non-profit institutions, by comparison, receive only 2.1 percent of their revenue from state governments, and a total of 17.1 percent from combined federal, state, and local government subsidies. The lack of state government funding is the price these institutions pay for their independence from the state government bureaucracy. The loss of this revenue is passed on to students and results in the significantly higher tuition prices at private institutions compared with public institutions.

For-profit institutions receive no revenue in the form of government subsidies and, as noted, pay taxes to the federal, state, and local governments. The for-profits earn 94.5 percent of their revenue from tuition, compared with an average of 18.4 percent for public non-profit institutions and 42.4 percent for private non-profit institutions. The other 5.5 percent of revenue for the for-profits comes from auxiliary enterprises (basically, the bookstore). No other sources of revenue exist in the for-profit institutions.

Interestingly, the for-profits do not attempt to expand their revenue

Table 4.1   Sources of Revenue for Institutions of Higher Education

Source of Revenue	Public Non-Profit	Private Non-Profit	For-Profit
Tuition and fees	18.4	42.4	94.5
Federal government	11.1	14.4	0
State government	35.9	2.1	0
Local government	4.0	0.6	0
Private gifts, grants, and contracts	4.0	8.8	0
Endowment income	0.6	4.7	0
Sales and services	23.1	22.2	5.5
Educational activities	3.0	2.8	0
Auxiliary enterprises	9.5	10.0	5.5
Hospitals	10.5	9.4	0
Other	3.1	4.7	0
Total	100.00	100.00	100.00

Sources: For the public and private non-profits, National Center for Education Statistics, *Digest of Educational Statistics* (1995). The For-Profit column was added by the author.

streams beyond that of tuition. They are content with being highly dependent on tuition as essentially their only source of revenue. In contrast, many traditional colleges and universities, especially the private, independent institutions, have been trying for years to get out from under their overdependence on tuition. Faced with rising costs and having reached the upper limits of what the market will bear in terms of tuition pricing, many traditional higher-education institutions in the United States have been attempting for many years to expand their sources of revenue beyond tuition. This effort has taken different forms, including the recent for-profit ventures in continuing education at Stanford, Columbia, New York University, Cornell, the University of Maryland, and Temple. Both public and private non-profit institutions have achieved some limited success in this effort, although the price of tuition has continued to escalate well above the rate of inflation for the past two decades.[29]

Tuition is viewed by the for-profit sector as being a more than adequate source of revenue to support current operations and generate profitability. In fact, compared with the sources of income in many other industries, tuition is a relatively stable and predictable foundation on which to build the financial security of the business. Because students return to continue their studies for several semesters, and pay their tuition prior to the actual delivery of their education, revenue can be accurately forecasted several years ahead.

Where the Money Goes

Directly comparing expenditures of for-profit institutions with those of non-profits is difficult because the budgeting and financial reporting practices differ widely. Non-profits, for example, use fund accounting, and for-profits do not. Consequently, the non-profits use expense categories for financial reporting that the for-profits do not use, such as separately defined line items for physical plant and library expenses. For-profits report how much they spend on such activities as selling and promotion (typically in the range of 10–15 percent of revenues), and non-profits do not. Depreciation of assets and provisions for taxes are important expense categories for the for-profits that the non-profits do not use. Consequently, a comparative analysis of the income statements and balance sheets of a for-profit university with those of a non-profit university involves a series of apples-and-oranges comparisons.

Nonetheless, in order to draw some useful distinctions, it is possible to make broad comparisons of where the money goes in the for-profits compared with in the non-profits. Some interesting similarities and differences are revealed by studying the financial reports of several of the for-profits, particularly the five profiled in this book—Apollo, DeVry, Education Management, Argosy, and Strayer—and comparing them with data available on the non-profits from such sources as the National Center for Higher Education Statistics.

While there are, as we have seen, some clear distinctions about the sources of revenue between the non-profits and the for-profits, there appear to be more similarities than differences in where the money goes. The largest single expenditure for all institutions is salaries, especially faculty salaries. William Jellema's classic study of college and university finances showed that faculty compensation consumes 50 percent or more of the budget at most non-profit colleges and universities.[30] The same appears to be true at the for-profits.

At Apollo, for instance, 59.6 percent of net revenue went for "instructional costs and services" in fiscal 1998. At DeVry the figure was 59 percent; at Education Management, 66 percent; at Argosy, 51 percent; and at Strayer, 39.6 percent.[31] In any educational enterprise based primarily on classroom instruction, the biggest expense is the salaries and benefits paid to the faculty. This holds true even at institutions that rely heavily on adjunct faculty, such as the University of Phoenix and Pace University, among many others. The increasing reliance on adjunct faculty at most colleges and universities may have stemmed the growth of the cost of faculty compensation, but this expense still accounts for the largest share of budgeted expenditures at most, if not all, institutions that hold regional association accreditation.

The salaries paid to faculty in these for-profit institutions are generally competitive with the salaries paid to faculty in non-profit institutions offering similar programs. I say generally because the strategy used by these institutions is to pay salaries that are "in the ballpark" but typically about 15 percent below what a candidate could get elsewhere. This strategy has the effect of creating significant salary savings in the aggregate while still attracting and retaining good candidates. At DeVry, for example, salary ranges for each faculty rank are reviewed annually against a sampling of salaries at other institutions in each region and against annual survey data, such as those reported in the *Chronicle of Higher Education*. Nine-month salaries have to be adjusted to eleven months in order to be comparable since all DeVry faculty teach the whole academic year, including summers.

Benefits are also generally competitive, but the TIAA-CREF retirement annuity program is not available at for-profit institutions. Instead, they offer faculty 401k retirement plans, which generally provide a lower-level institutional contribution to faculty retirement accounts. To help offset this, the big for-profits offer faculty stock options in the form of bonuses and rewards for outstanding performance.

Thus, while faculty compensation is generally a bit lower at for-profit institutions, these institutions are able to compete for faculty looking for a more corporate working environment, and one where there is no pressure to publish. There is no evidence that the leading for-profit institutions are having difficulty hiring and retaining faculty because the compensation is too low.

After faculty compensation, the next biggest expense category at non-profit institutions is "general administrative," which includes the cost of the central administrative functions, such as administrator and staff salaries and benefits and expenses for offices that serve the whole institution, such as student services and the placement office. At most non-profits, these expenses typically consume about 25 percent of budgeted expenditures.[32]

One would expect the for-profits to spend less on general administrative expenses, given the higher level of accountability and efficiency expected in these business organizations. Indeed, this appears to be true. Apollo spent only 9.8 percent of revenues for "general and administrative" in fiscal 1998; DeVry, 13.4 percent; Education Management, 22.3 percent; and Strayer, 14.4 percent.[33] This is one of the areas of cost containment in which the for-profits have been able to capitalize, figuratively and literally. The administrative and management ranks are leaner in these organizations than in the non-profits. The work of the administrative staff, including the academic deans, is more closely supervised in these environments, in which all managers are held accountable for results. The limited and highly focused missions of these institutions also means that the work of administrators is more focused.

The for-profits spend little or nothing on programs and activities that are not directly related to the students' educational experience in classrooms and instructional laboratories. Most of the for-profits have no student residences, for example, or sports teams, and while they do not realize any revenue from these kinds of activities, they also do not carry any of the expenses.

There is one other area of significant difference in the budgeted expenditures of the for-profits compared with the non-profits: provision for taxes. Apollo, DeVry, Education Management, Argosy, and Strayer each set aside about 40 percent of their earnings before taxes for paying taxes. Non-profit colleges and universities do not pay any taxes and therefore do not have to budget for this expense.

Aside from the notable differences in spending on general administrative expenses and taxes, the budgeted expenditures of the non-profits and the for-profits are not strikingly different. Perhaps a fundamental distinction between these sectors lies in how the financial resources of the institutions are managed, which is reflected, in part, in the financial performance of the leading for-profit universities.

Financial Performance of the For-Profits

As a newly rediscovered sector of what analysts call the knowledge-based economy, the for-profit providers of higher education have not only attracted billions of dollars of private investment capital; they have also made significant improvements in academic quality, as indicated by their meeting regional and professional accreditation standards. As mentioned earlier, during the latter half of the 1990s for-profit educational companies raised more than $4.8 billion in equity capital through more than 40 initial public offerings and as many follow-on offerings.[34] This remarkable level of investment activity attests to a changed public perception of proprietary education in the United States, as well as the attractive financial performance of these companies. Wall Street investment houses remain bullish on education companies, encouraging their investors to include them as a standard industry category in their investment portfolios. Many investment analysts and industry watchers predict a continued shift of public funds for education into private enterprise for at least the next decade.[35]

One the key indicators of the financial performance of the five largest for-profit providers is how quickly they can manage to realize profits from a new campus, location, or acquisition. Each of these companies, but particularly Apollo, Strayer, and DeVry, is adding new campuses every year. DeVry's corporate plan is to open two to three new campuses each year for the next ten years, each one built on the basic DeVry model of a 125,000-square-foot facility capable of handling about 3,600 students. Apollo's corporate plan is even more aggressive, with a "start-up ramp" sufficient to sustain revenue growth of at least 30 percent each year.[36] Both companies operate new campuses and instructional locations at a loss for the first three or four semesters before breaking even and making them profitable. By the second year of operation, a new DeVry campus is generating profit, and Apollo has recently trimmed the break-even point to less than one year.[37]

Table 4.2 summarizes several metrics of financial performance for the five largest higher-education companies. Together, these five com-

Table 4.2 Financial Performance for Selected For-Profit Providers

Company	Stock Performance 1994–1999	P/E Ratios		P/E/G		5-Year Estimated Growth	Default Rate	Placement Rate
		1998	1999	1998	1999			
Apollo Group	1538%	32.7	25.9	139%	109%	30%	5.8%	—[a]
DeVry University	743%	53.1	42.6	309%	265%	20%	17.0%	96%
Education Management[b]	269%	42.1	35.0	245%	210%	20%	16.6%	87%
ITT Educational Services	710%	35.3	29.3	212%	176%	20%	17.2%	90%
Strayer Education	399%	27.7	22.5	—	—	20%	15.2%	79%

Sources: Primarily company records and industry reports esp. Merrill Lynch, *In-Depth Report: The Book of Knowledge, Investing in the Growing Education and Training Industry,* Report 1268 (9 April 1999); and, H. Block, ed., *Education Industry Overview: The E-Bang Theory,* Banc of America Securities, Illuminismo Volume 2, Education Industry Overview (September 1999).

[a]Not applicable, because most of the students at Apollo are already employed.
[b]ITT is substituted for Argosy in this table because Argosy became a public company in 1999, and a history of financial performance data is not yet available. However, Argosy's default rate in 1999 was 4.6%, and its placement rate was 95%.

panies represent approximately 275 college campuses and a total enrollment of about 225,000 students. Collectively, the number of campuses and students has been growing annually at a rate close to 20
percent.

There are several different ways of looking at the financial performance of these companies, and all of them indicate financial health and
probable future growth. One simple metric is the five-year history of
stock performance, shown in the first column of table 4.2. The growth
of the price of the stock of these companies has been impressive and is
an indicator of both profitability and consumer confidence in the future of for-profit higher education. The P/E (price/earnings) multiple
ratios and the P/E/G (price/earnings/growth) percentages, shown in
columns 2 and 3, are also very favorable indicators of the financial health
of these companies. The five-year estimated growth, in column 4, suggests year-over-year estimated growth estimates in the range of 20–30
percent, which is excellent.

Another indicator of the financial performance and financial accountability of the most prominent for-profit colleges and universities is the
default rates on student loans, shown in column 5. These percentages
are at or below the national average of approximately 17 percent for all
institutions.[38] There was a time, in the mid-1970s, when default rates
on student loans for proprietary school students was much higher, in
the 25–30 percent range. Supporters of non-profit higher education
heavily criticized proprietary schools for these high rates, and some
suggested that students in for-profit schools should be ineligible for
federally sponsored student loans. The DOE studied the matter and
found that high default rates generally were not the fault of the institutions themselves but correlated with the socioeconomic profile of the
students, particularly race, family income, and low wages. One such
study concluded: "The use of absolute default rates as a condition of
eligibility for student aid could therefore penalize those schools that
enroll students with a higher propensity to default: minorities, economically disadvantaged students, and students whose training is in
low-wage fields."[39] As the relatively low default rates in table 4.2 indicate, the leading for-profit institutions have found ways to manage default rates for student loans. They have done this by providing better
service to students and lenders and closely supervising student-loan

accounts. However, a portion of the approximately 7,000 proprietary schools in the United States probably continue to have high default rates, as do historically black colleges and community colleges enrolling a high percentage of students with developmental needs.

Career-placement rates are another indicator of financial performance in the for-profits. As noted earlier, placement drives the whole enterprise, ensuring market demand and continuing enrollment growth. At DeVry, Education Management, and Argosy, placement rates have been at or close to 90 percent for more than a decade. Many other proprietary institutions also excel in the area of placement.

As good as they are, however, the high placement rates of for-profit institutions raise some fundamental questions, chief among them the question whether these institutions are truly providing students with a college education or just offering training in preparation for work. We will consider this question in the chapters that follow.

5

The Academic Culture of For-Profit Universities

Making a Profit off the Backs of Students

During a recent public hearing in New Jersey at which a for-profit university was proposing to offer a new bachelor's-degree program, one non-profit college president openly asked the president of the for-profit institution, "So tell me, just how much profit do you make off the backs of your students?"

This statement reveals the fear among traditional educators that the for-profits are doing harm to higher education and to students. It probably also reveals frustration that the for-profits are growing, multiplying, and gaining market share at a time when some non-profit colleges are struggling to stay open. Presumably the for-profits are able to do this, at least in part, at the expense of the faculty, who are not protected by tenure and who, it is assumed, have little academic freedom. However, the statement also reveals, in suggesting that profit is being made "off the backs of students," a persistent judgment of for-profit higher-education institutions that is based, in the words of Jonathan Fife in his introduction to a 1990 ASHE-ERIC study of proprietary schools, "on surface impressions and general misunderstanding."[1] Those who live and work inside for-profit universities are keenly aware of this judgment on the part of colleagues in traditional institutions.

As we saw in chapter 3, for-profit educational ventures in America have been viewed with great suspicion by many traditional educators since the colonial era. Advertisements that seem to promise too much, admissions standards based on the ability to pay, and curricula that appear to oversimplify subject matter all have fueled this suspicion. Without doubt some of the criticism levied against proprietary schools has been deserved. As the educational historian Edmund James wrote in 1900, the for-profit school "embodies all the defects and the excellencies of the American character."[2]

Today, the word *proprietary*, an innocent enough term that refers to ownership by a proprietor, still has a sharply negative edge to it. *Proprietary* has been associated with fly-by-night correspondence schools and inside-the-matchbook-cover promotions. The profit motive, which involves charging more for a product or service than it actually costs, is thought to be essentially incompatible with an educational mission. "If they are organized on a proprietary basis and are run for profit," said officials of the fledgling National Educational Association in 1938, "they have no place in our system of education."[3]

If for-profit schools are making profits, especially when tax-subsidized institutions struggle to break even, it is usually assumed that they are doing so by cutting corners that should not be cut and by duping unsuspecting student customers into believing that they are going to get something they are not. "Educational philosophers," wrote Herbert Tonne in a 1938 article responding to the NEA's indictment of the for-profits, "seem to be coming to the conclusion that any constructive work which results in a profit has an inherent element of wickedness in it."[4] This conclusion apparently persists today in the minds of many traditional educators.

In contrast, business people do not mistrust the profit motive, and they tend to understand immediately what for-profit universities are all about. Yet many business leaders are baffled by the inner workings of a non-profit university; it makes no sense to them. Scott Cowen, president of Tulane University, who is a former business school dean with a

Ph.D. in accounting, puts it this way: "The way most universities are organized and conduct their operations defies logic and common sense."[5] Anyone who has worked with the trustees of non-profit universities knows how many of the trustees struggle to understand the culture of the traditional academic institution.

Understanding a for-profit university involves knowing something about its academic and management culture. Unless you live and work in a for-profit educational environment, it is almost impossible to know this culture from the perspective of traditional higher education. The world of for-profit higher education is a unique environment that combines the hard edges of American capitalism and the altruistic vision of an educational institution serving society. For readers who have never set foot inside a for-profit university, I hope to provide a guided tour of what it's like to live and work in these institutions from my perspective as someone who is also intimately familiar with the culture of several non-profits. There are cultural characteristics unique to for-profit universities, such as the blending of business management with academic pursuits, the shift in the balance of power toward students and away from faculty, and the absence of tenure and its affect on academic freedom.

Until recently, very few educators had crossed the career boundary between non-profit and proprietary higher education. The literature on the culture of academic institutions makes little or no reference to the for-profits, and attempts to create typologies of organizational cultures in academia, such as W. H. Bergquest's *Four Cultures of the Academy*, do not mention for-profit institutions.[6]

Put simply, an organization's culture is an artifact of the shared values, attitudes, priorities, and practices of its members, and especially of its leaders. Its culture is particularly revealed in the nature of relationships between people in the organization. In Latin, the term *culture* means cultivation, or tilling of the soil, which nicely captures the dynamic and changing nature of an organization's culture.

The Cultural Tightrope: Balancing Business and Academics

As I said, for-profit universities are unique organizational blends of business enterprise and academic institution. At the classroom level they look and behave like traditional colleges, but as you move up the organizational hierarchy in the for-profits, they look and feel more like businesses and less like academic institutions. For-profit presidents resemble traditional CEOs more than they are do academic leaders. They are focused on planning, on setting and implementing institutional strategy, and especially on the managing of resources and operations.

The management culture in for-profit universities is decidedly conservative. Despite their reputation for market aggressiveness, the for-profits are usually characterized by simple, tried-and-true management techniques. Because higher education was one of the few industries in the United States to escape the industrial revolution and is today perhaps the last large American industry to adopt modern management principles, simple management approaches have a profound impact on operational efficiency and profitability.[7] The successful for-profits in America today, including the large corporate structures like Apollo, DeVry, Education Management, Strayer, and Argosy, are run according to basic meat-and-potatoes management practices, such as management by objectives, close supervision of work, incremental budgeting, progressive discipline, and detailed oversight of local operations by the home office.

Management and staff employees working in these organizations find that there is an extraordinary emphasis on the details. Exact and precise records are maintained each semester on all aspects of academic operations that affect the business, from classroom utilization to grade distributions by course. Exhaustingly detailed records are maintained regarding student financial aid, an area in which the for-profits take pains to be squeaky-clean. This focus on details is another aspect of the for-profit response to a higher-education industry in which business details have often been neglected.

Their dual nature—part business and part academic institution—is one of the distinguishing features of for-profit universities. Figure 5.1 illustrates the differences in how the dual cultures of business and academics are balanced in for-profit and non-profit universities. In the for-profits, at the levels of the board, the president, the provost, and the academic deans the dominant culture is business. The language of business is used at these levels to describe organizational activity, to discuss initiatives, and to measure results. In the non-profits, the dominant conversation at these levels tends to center more on academics and less on business. The deans, the provost, and even the president at non-profits tend to use the language of academics to describe and measure organizational activity. Of course, the two cultures are interwoven to some extent; they are not always distinct. As well, the academic side of the non-profits has for some years been increasingly adapting the language of business, especially in the area of marketing. In general, however, the distinction in figure 5.1 holds true, reflecting different priorities and the different hierarchies of values within for-profit and non-profit institutions, as discussed in chapter 1.

For example, one of the ultimate priorities of the publicly held for-profit university can be described in the simplest of terms as growth in market share. As long as market share increases, the financial health of

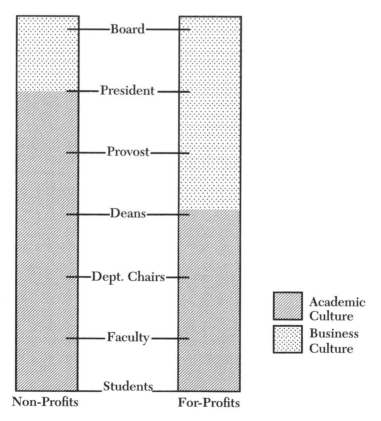

Fig. 5.1   Balance of the Dual Cultures

the enterprise is assured and academic quality is financially protected. In contrast, one of the ultimate priorities of the non-profit college or university can be described as the security and growth of its academic reputation, for this is what assures the institution a continuing sense of its rightful place in the tradition of the academy and allows the institution to continue to attract not only students and faculty but also income in the form of donations and grants.

At the level of the classroom, however, for-profit universities have the ethos of typical academic institutions. If you woke up and found yourself in a classroom at a for-profit university, you would probably not be able to tell the difference between it and a typical college classroom. There would be nothing particularly unusual about the setting, the physical space, or the behavior of students and faculty. Many of the for-profits, especially those with degree programs that focus on high-technology fields such as telecommunications, information systems, electronics, and health care, annually invest significant resources in instructional technology, so you might notice more and newer computer equipment in the classrooms and laboratories. Nevertheless, even this would not be very different from the situation at a well-funded public university or private college. If the class you woke up in was a general education course, say, introduction to psychology, you would not be able to tell any difference between it and a similar course taught at other colleges.

If anything else struck you about the classroom, it might be that the room itself is tidier than many typical college classrooms. The chairs and tables would be in neat rows, with little or no trash lying around. If you looked out the window of your classroom, you would see that the grounds, though small, and the parking areas, though large, are clean and well maintained. At for-profit college the lawns will always be mowed, the snow always plowed (or the palm fronds trimmed), and the restrooms always cleaned, for it is part of corporate culture to do so. Because they are businesses in a service industry, most of the for-profits pay great attention to facilities maintenance, grounds, and housekeeping. Even if faced with revenue losses, most of the for-profit companies would probably not compromise facilities and maintenance.

If you woke up and found yourself in a for-profit faculty meeting, you might notice some differences. Nearly all the faculty would be in attendance, and they would arrive on time. They would probably know one another because they probably work in the same building, and while there would be a few new faces in the crowd, there would be many familiar faces. Typically, more than half of the faculty would have been employed there full time for five years or more, and half of them for ten or more years.

Faculty colleagues at the for-profit campus might appear to be somewhat more polite and reserved in their interactions with one another and with administrators than those at traditional universities. Without a system of tenure, and teaching in a work environment in which annual reviews are performance-based, faculty in the for-profits are at-will employees like everyone else. Faculty have no special job protection beyond that of other nonexempt employees, and they serve "at the will" of their employer. While there is a system of faculty rank from instructor to full professor (some for-profits add the fifth rank of senior professor), senior faculty generally do not evaluate the work of junior faculty for purposes of promotion. Faculty rank, therefore, tends to have less influence on relationships between colleagues in the for-profit environment.

The curriculum is managed centrally by professional curriculum specialists, so the faculty here engage in fewer ideological debates about the curriculum, the number of credit hours required in their fields as opposed to others, and the direction of the college's curriculum development. Still, you would witness lively conversation about subject matter and students and hear passionately held opinions about teaching methods. Conversation about teaching would probably reflect a fairly sophisticated level of thought about what it means to be a teacher, how to manage a classroom, and how to reach today's students. Most of the for-profit faculty would be teaching three or four courses a term, and some would be teaching one or two lab sections in addition. The standard teaching load for full-time faculty at most for-profits is equivalent to 12 hours at a traditional university, with some faculty teaching up to 15 hours a semester and some as few as six. Some faculty are given reductions in teaching load for performing administrative work, curriculum development projects, and completion of Ph.D. dissertations. Most faculty teach four days a week. The pace is typically rather incessant, however, with classes running year round, days, evenings and weekends, usually in three 15-week semesters with only a week or two off between semesters.

There would be relatively less conversation among faculty about research and scholarship since these areas are typically secondary or absent in the mission of the for-profit university. Some of the faculty would engage in scholarship anyway because they were trained to do so and because it is an expression of who they are as educators and thinkers. Some would be working on their Ph.D, either at the dissertation stage or still in coursework, and they would be receiving tuition reimbursement and probably a teaching-load reduction. Nearly all the faculty, including some of the general-education specialists, would have significant industry experience at the professional level, several with 20 years of work experience. Many would also have years of teaching experience at traditional colleges and universities, and some would be casualties of traditional academic department politics and university-wide promotion-and-tenure committees. Some would be anticipating an upcoming sabbatical, since some of the for-profits are making substantial investments in the professional development of faculty, including sabbaticals every five years, generous support for travel, special funding for instructional technology, and a system that allows faculty to "bank" some of their teaching hours and then cash them in by taking a semester off from teaching.

Moving up the organizational hierarchy, if you found yourself in a deans'-council meeting, you would know rather quickly that you were not in traditional academe. Conversation would be focused on the numbers—retention rates, completion projections, grade distributions, failure rates by course, and so forth. Of course, such conversation is increasingly apparent in the non-profits as well, as is discussion about new program ideas and curriculum development. Perhaps the biggest difference here would be the use of words like *product mix*, and even *sales*, alongside the more familiar *pedagogy* and *learning community*.

Pivotal Role of the Academic Dean

At the dean's level is where the distinguishing and dynamic tension between business and academe is most strongly felt. "The dean is the bridge between the business side and the academic side," notes Eli Schwartz, a faculty member and former dean at the Chicago campus of the American Schools of Professional Psychology, owned by the Argosy Education Group.[8] This bridging role of the dean appears to hold true for most, perhaps all, of the for-profit institutions. The deans are part academic leaders and part business managers, with most of the emphasis on the latter. You would probably notice a high level of teamwork among them, for they have a strong sense of common objectives and, more importantly, do not have to compete with one another for resources. The allocation of resources is negotiated once each year and is based strictly on needs that are justified in the language of business. The approval of new faculty positions, for example, depends on documented enrollment increases and student demand for classes, not on academic- or discipline-based arguments. Political positioning and turf battles are not the essence of deaning in this environment. Their biggest challenge is finding the right balance between the dual roles of academic leader and business manager responsible for making the numbers, particularly the retention and completion rates of students in their programs.

Table 5.1 compares some of the roles of academic deans in the for-profit and non-profit sectors. In the non-profits, for example, an academic dean typically devotes much of his or her energy to representing the interests and concerns of the faculty to senior administrators and to outside groups, often including potential donors. In such situations the dean speaks for the faculty and is expected to articulate the shared vision of the faculty. In contrast, the for-profit dean is more concerned with supervising the work of the faculty (a concept that will be explored more fully below). Similarly, the non-profit dean is usually in competition with other deans to increase and maintain financial support for programs, while the for-profit dean is more focused on the implementation of resources that have already been allocated in preparation for launching new academic programs. In the latter case, the for-profit dean's challenge is not to secure a fair share of resources but to put to effective use resources that have already been committed. In addition, whereas the non-profit dean is often concerned with protecting turf, the for-profit dean is more concerned with managing change. Finally, the for-profit dean is required to provide ongoing measures of student academic performance and satisfaction, both of which are seen as vital to the health of the business and, ultimately, to academic quality.

Table 5.1   Roles of Academic Deans at Non-Profit and
For-Profit Institutions

Non-Profit Dean	For-Profit Dean
Representing the faculty to inside and outside groups	Supervising the work of the faculty
Maintaining support for existing academic programs	Managing the launching of new academic programs
Protecting turf	Managing rapid change
Providing justification for the allocation of new resources	Measuring student performance and satisfaction

Certainly, such distinctions are not absolute and will vary among in-stitutional environments. In general, however, the non-profit dean is an advocate, a strategist, and a politician, while the for-profit dean is an academic manager who is caught in the middle of the dynamic tension between the business and academic sides of the enterprise.

As a chief academic officer at a for-profit college, I often feel caught in this tension—some would call it conflict—myself. Like all academic leaders, I am expected to articulate and defend the values of teaching, learning, and, to a lesser extent, scholarly inquiry. I am the head cheer-leader for high academic standards and excellence in teaching. I am expected to notice and encourage creativity and innovation in the class-room. In addition, I am the business manager who is held accountable for results, including making the numbers on such things as continu-ous improvement in student retention and completion rates, along with meeting targets for average class sizes and even ensuring reasonably consistent grade distributions among faculty members teaching the same courses. I am expected to develop accurate forecasts for several key performance indicators and report regularly on performance against goals. When push comes to shove, I need to deliver results like any manager in a business organization. If I do not, it will be reflected as poor performance in my annual performance review.

Academic Voice at the Top

One of the peculiar challenges of working in this kind of for-profit environment, especially for those who, like me, come from traditional academic cultures, is that the senior managers, notably the institution presidents and those to whom they report, are basically operational managers and not academic leaders. This is especially the case in publicly traded companies that own and operate multiple campuses. Their first accountability is managing the bottom line, the primary number being the gross profit margin. At the corporate level, the regional vice presidents and other senior executives are business people, not academic types.

As a result, the academic voice at the top of these companies is silent, or at best a whisper. This is not unlike the relationship between many traditional colleges and universities and their boards of trustees, which are, for the most part, made up of business people who themselves lack a context for appreciating cumbersome academic decision-making processes and what they sometimes perceive as academic whining. The difference, I think, is that trustees can be managed, or at least to some extent intimidated, controlled, or otherwise humored. However, when the bosses are business people who do not have a Ph.D and who bring a pragmatic and straightforward approach to supervising the work of professional teachers and scholars, it changes the nature of academic conversation within the institution.

A discussion about effective teaching, for example, is basically reduced to a conversation about grade distributions, failure rates, withdrawal rates, and student progression to the next-level course, rather than, say, a conversation about teaching people how to think critically. If these more pedestrian measures show results that are deemed acceptable by management, then the conversation can proceed to the more philosophical, discipline-based issues of teaching, learning, and pedagogy. Curriculum conversations too are centered first on how the arrangement of courses contributes to students' success in completing the program. Such discipline-based issues as whether students should take microeconomics before macroeconomics, or financial accounting before managerial accounting, are grounded in the question of what contributes to student success rather than in the questions of what constitutes correct discipline and proper tradition. These kinds of shifts in the nature of academic conversation within the institution stem in large measure from the fact that most of the institutional power is held by the business side.

It is tempting to cite the lack of academic voice at the top as one of the fatal flaws of the publicly held for-profit education companies, a weakness that will eventually lead to a serious disregard for academic standards. Indeed, when the North Central Association of Colleges and Schools visited the DeVry system for a 10-year review in 1992, they ended up granting renewal of accreditation, but with a required focus visit in five years. One of the concerns cited in the 1992 North Central report was the lack of "integration of the academic perspective into the organizational structure." I myself have complained on occasion about the lack of academic perspective at the top within the DeVry system, but I have also come to realize that the tension and occasional conflict between the business and academic sides can be a healthy dynamic. This tension often protects the financial health of the enterprise, and financial health is necessary to sustain academic quality in all institutions. Having spent 20 years as an academic dean in public, private, and liberal arts settings, I know that there are also serious weaknesses in the traditional model, in which the academic perspective is evident at the top of the administrative hierarchy. I have worked for presidents and provosts who could speak eloquently about scholarly work and academic disciplines but could not perform as good managers or effective leaders. In my experience, the traditional academic culture places so much emphasis on the value of collaboration and consensus that the importance of timely decision making is often pushed to the background. In the name of "creating a dialogue among stakeholders" the emphasis too often shifts away from making forthright decisions to settling for default decisions because they are the least troublesome to the loudest voices in the academic community. In fact, a president or provost who is strategic and decisive is often feared and sometimes despised by the faculty. The culture of the non-profits encourages leaders to cultivate accommodating social skills and to reach compromises, but it does not necessarily encourage them to make clear decisions that improve teaching, learning, and the future of the institution.

Both non-profits and for-profits care about both academic quality and a healthy bottom line. The difference is that the for-profits change the center of gravity by radically shifting the balance between academics and business in favor of sound business practices. The for-profit president is first and foremost a business executive, expected to exercise managerial control over all operations and make day-to-day decisions.

The faculty in the for-profits are the center of the academic life of the organization, but they do not run the institution or even hold most of the power. They are the skilled workhorses in the for-profit system. They teach the curriculum assigned to them. They participate in curriculum development, but they do not make the final decisions regarding the curriculum. Nor are they directly involved in the recruitment and admission of students, as these functions are handled entirely by professionals trained in marketing and sales.

Faculty as Delivery People

In a real sense, faculty in the for-profits are viewed by the business side as being delivery people, as in delivery of the curriculum. The delivery mode in almost all the for-profit universities is classroom-based, with distance learning being a small part of the operation. At the University of Phoenix, which many people mistakenly think is an online institution, fewer than 7 percent of the 100,000 students are pursuing their degrees via distance learning.[9] Similarly, at DeVry, Education Management, Strayer, and most others, distance learning is used only to supplement instruction in the accelerated and weekend programs, in which the bulk of instruction still occurs in the classroom. The perception within the for-profits of faculty as delivery people is built primarily upon the traditional model of classroom-based instruction.

This view may be especially apparent in the opening of new for-profit campuses, where a manufacturing approach is usually applied to the start-up process. "They have the idea," says one for-profit dean, referring to the home-office executives, "that once the building is ready, all we need to do is drive up with a truck load of laborers (faculty), hand them textbooks and curriculum guides, and bingo, let them teach."[10] Intellectual passion, disciplinary specialty, and deep engagement with material are not particularly well understood by the business side. Teaching is viewed as a fundamentally straightforward activity involving artful presentation of material, repetition of key concepts, and reinforcement of learning through testing and grading. This is seen by the business side as the basic work of the faculty. When it comes to making business decisions that affect the for-profit higher-education company, the faculty are not considered experts, and their input and authority are limited.

In fact, faculty who want to advance ideas that will require resources must not only demonstrate their academic value but also show that they are sound business innovations. The discipline of couching academic ideas in business terms radically changes the nature of conversations in an academic setting. Suddenly there is a greater need to be accountable for the welfare of the whole institution—for its financial health as well as its academic quality. Strong feelings about how things "should be" are insufficient bases for decision making or even serious conversation. If a member of the faculty feels passionately about the need for smaller classes, for example, that passion must be accompanied by a rational argument and some hard evidence showing why smaller classes are a good business decision. If the argument is that smaller classes result in more effective learning and better student retention, evidence must be provided to back up these claims. Of course, the faculty are free to debate these kinds of issues at length in faculty meetings and committees. Any formal proposal for change, however, must include a justification grounded in the language and culture of business before it will be taken seriously by the business side.

The greater emphasis on the business side is especially apparent in the lack of a tenure system at for-profit universities. This essential difference is worth looking at in some detail, for the absence of the tenure system is a fundamental distinction between the academic culture of for-profit institutions and that of non-profit institutions.

Living without Tenure

Freed from the system of tenure, for-profit universities are able to address what James Coleman has called the basic structural fault of the traditional university: that faculty members are granted the rights of membership in a community without the normative constraints that such a community would usually require and that they have all the rights of an employee of a corporation, including the security of salary and employment benefits, without the obligation to surrender control of their time for the pursuit of a corporate goal.[11] Without tenure, the faculty are professional, exempt employees, and while this has obvious benefit in terms of employment flexibility for the university, it also quite naturally raises questions about the quality of the working lives of the faculty.

Though they do not have tenure, many for-profit faculty find that they have some notable freedoms under the corporate structure. A number of the faculty I interviewed on the campuses of Argosy, Strayer, DeVry, and Education Management said they felt that they had at least as much academic freedom as they had had when they taught at traditional universities; a few actually said they had more. Several commented on the freedom in the classroom that seems to result from an institutional emphasis on teaching rather than research, and they said that in the for-profit environment the primacy of teaching is not merely politically correct catalog copy but reality. Other faculty noted the lack of pressure from other faculty members to teach certain subjects in a particular way. Because the for-profits are run by business people, who typically have little or no firsthand experience as faculty and generally lack a sophisticated understanding of education at the classroom level, creative members of the faculty appear to find considerable room to shape the academic culture. "We can create never-before-heard-of committees," said one member of a for-profit institution's general-education faculty, a Ph.D. in literature. "We can recommend special elective and honors courses, work the system to hire the people we want to, do our own research as we see fit, and have a life beyond academe." Some of the faculty I talked with emphasized that they can turn to their colleagues for insight and support and not be fearful of them as competitors. "We can develop ourselves in the direction we'd like to go," said one, adding, "You can't do that at traditional institutions when you are scrambling for tenure, or post-tenure review, or trying to get promoted."[12]

Tenure's primary purpose has always been to protect academic freedom: to ground the concept of academic freedom by providing protection from sanction in the exercise of free speech and the pursuit of knowledge. Tenure is a means of giving operational definition to the idea of academic freedom within the social system and hierarchy of values of the university. It sets professors apart and gives them privileged status. This privileged social status is sanctioned by the high esteem society in general attributes to the activities of teaching, research, and learning in cultured society.

Tenure's loudest critics used to be those outside the academy—journalists, legislators, business and civic leaders—who perhaps did not understand the particular heritage and nature of higher education as only an insider can. It was fairly easy to dismiss their views as uninformed and misguided. However, in recent years some of the noisiest calls for elimination of the tenure system have come from inside academe. Trampling on sacred ground, these detractors have tended to choose their language carefully, as if to say, "Tenure is a perfectly lovely idea; it just doesn't work in its present form." Peter Magrath, for example, a political scientist, former state-university president, and head of the National Association of State Universities and Land-Grant Colleges, is one of the current leaders within the traditional system who admits that tenure "has become more of a problem than a help in our endeavors."[13] Magrath suggests that the tenure system may have become a deterrent, rather than a contribution, to the overall health of higher education in America.

Other insiders have come to share this view, including some with a breadth and depth of experience that makes it difficult to casually dismiss their views as misguided. For example, Richard Chait, of the Harvard School of Education, was for years the administrator of Harvard's noted Institute for Education Management, a summer training program for emerging leaders in colleges and universities. Fueled by a million-dollar grant from the Pew Charitable Trust, Chait and his associates are completing research on tenure and its alternatives that appears to be headed toward the conclusions that the current tenure system may be dysfunctional and that a growing number of members of the professoriate think that it should be abolished.[14]

It is one thing to study tenure, to conduct surveys, and to do historical and philosophical analyses of the concept, and quite another to actually run a successful college without a system of tenure. The absence of tenure at for-profit universities is one of the reasons why their rapid growth troubles many of those who want to retain tenure. The for-profits are clearly different from the non-profits in terms of the narrower scope of academic mission they pursue, but they nevertheless demonstrate that academia can work quite successfully without tenure. Removing tenure means removing one of the major sources of academic struggle and lack of accountability within the traditional university.

I am delighted that in my work as an academic dean at DeVry I no longer have to deal with tenure. The absence of tenure means that I can treat my faculty as professional associates and actually hold my faculty colleagues accountable for doing their jobs, and gain their respect in doing so. After years of managerial impotence in traditional universities, it is incredibly satisfying to be able to do something about an incompetent teacher. Handled with respect and professionalism, such interventions with the poorest performers can actually strengthen the total faculty's confidence in their academic leaders without violating anyone's academic freedom.

Not too long ago, for example, I removed a faculty member from the classroom in the middle of the semester and placed him on medical leave. Students in this person's classes had complained that he would launch into long, personal stories that seemed to have nothing to do with the topic at hand. After making two classroom visits, the chair of the department suggested that the faculty member seemed to be having difficulty concentrating and would sometimes appear to utterly lose his place in the material. Two of his colleagues, including his office mate, stopped by my office to express concern that he seemed increasingly confused and withdrawn. Another faculty member was deeply offended by him because he apparently accosted her verbally in front of her students. It became clear to me that the academic community for which I was responsible was becoming increasingly concerned about this situation.

When I initially talked with the faculty member, I was careful to be direct but not accusatory. His first response was to become defensive, to deny that anything was wrong, and to voice his personal resentment about the unnecessary visits to his classroom. During a meeting in my office the next day, however, he seemed placid and agreeable. He said that he was going through a difficult time and had been taking different medications for "an emotional situation." When I empathized with him, he opened up even more and invited me to talk with his psychiatrist, which I did by telephone. The psychiatrist confirmed that there was a problem in finding the right medication and dosage, and at my request, he faxed me a brief letter to that effect. A day later, before the next class meeting, I decided to place this person on medical leave and made arrangements for someone else to take over his classes.

I did not consult with anyone except the human-resources director and my president before making this decision. The students were satisfied with our responsiveness. Other members of the faculty expressed gratitude that the problem had been addressed quickly and without fanfare. The faculty member himself wrote to me sometime later and said he felt greatly relieved to be out of the classroom for a while.

What I find unusual about this case is that the faculty member's initial resistance did not deter the process of coming to an efficient resolution. This probably would not have been the case in the traditional environment of tenure and due process, which often have the effect of preventing quick action.

It must be said that one consequence of tenure is the protection of those who do not need protection. The best faculty—the gifted teachers, thoughtful and productive scholars, and those who truly give of themselves to their institutions—do not need the job security that tenure provides. Tenure does not free them to be productive and successful, for they would be productive and successful anyway. The worst faculty—those who dislike their students, have little institutional loyalty, and scarcely contribute to scholarly work—are the ones that tenure often protects. While this group does not constitute the majority of tenured faculty, every institution has its share of them, and their presence often has a poisonous effect on the whole enterprise.

The employment practices at the for-profits recognize that a person's individual performance may, and usually does, change in some ways over the years, just as institutions change. This is a fact of employment life in all professions, and higher education is no exception. Such change is not a bad thing; it is just inevitable and often hard. The hard part is that some people are simply not as valuable to the institution today as they were ten or twenty years ago. People get tired, burn out, or grow lazy and grumpy. The college's agenda changes because of demographic and economic realities, and the norms change. Faculty who were hired years ago may be confronted with new rules about scholarly productivity, professional involvement, the uses of instructional technology, and what constitutes good teaching. Curriculum content, teaching technologies, and bodies of knowledge change.

To their credit, many faculty respond to these challenges by rising to the occasion and getting themselves up to speed. However, on virtually every campus that has a tenure system some faculty hide behind the tenure they earned years ago and are reluctant to embrace changes that threaten the status quo. Since there is no real incentive for them to change, they hinder their institution's ability to respond effectively to change. Innovation and creativity are stifled, and some areas of the curriculum may become intellectual cemeteries. Responding effectively to the changing needs and demands of students, to employers of graduates, and even to changes in the disciplines themselves is imperative for today's universities.

The privileged status tenure affords has sometimes been abused, not just by members of the professoriate but also by deans, provosts, and presidents who have been more interested in being well liked than in making hard and right decisions. The shortcomings of tenure are also the result of the failure of administrators to properly manage the system in the first place.

It must also be said that tenure has sometimes been used as a tool for denying the academic freedom of those who do not have it, especially junior faculty. Because the tenured faculty have considerable control over the tenure-granting process, junior faculty sometimes get caught in departmental politics, old resentments among senior faculty, and battles over turf that have nothing to do with their value as candidates for tenure. "Fortunately," writes Lennard Davis in his essay "The Uses of Fear and Envy in Academe," "murder is still fairly rare in academe, but enough backstabbing goes on in the profession to put Jacobean tragedy to shame."[15] His statement refers to the Oxford don who a few years ago took action against a rival professor by killing him—an extreme instance of the academy as snake pit rather than ivory tower. Yet junior faculty sometimes get sacrificed for any number of real or imagined crimes.

In hopes of sifting through to the root causes of these issues, some commentators have argued that the real problem with tenure is bad hiring decisions in the first place—that the wrong faculty get on search committees and select weaker candidates who are less intellectually threatening to them.[16] The process of screening job applicants, especially when it is handled by a committee of vested interests, can be imperfect and subjective. It is interesting to note that the for-profit institutions profiled in this book generally do not use search committees to fill faculty positions. Instead, the dean makes these appointments, sometimes with considerable input from others and sometimes with none. Still, some candidates who present themselves well during the interview process and seem a good fit later turn out to be bad hiring decisions. In other cases, a candidate who is hired over the reservations and objections of some members of the search committee turns out to be a good hiring decision. However, these are probably failings of the hiring process, not of tenure. Tenure's basic objective, it seems, is to protect academic freedom.

The Meaning of Academic Freedom

In America, the idea of academic freedom was controversial right from the start. In 1915 the American Association of University Professors (AAUP) was established by a committee of senior professors who came up with the first official statement on academic freedom and tenure for the American professoriate. The *New York Times* responded in a critical editorial, noting, "Many sins are committed in the name of academic freedom," and arguing that "free speech is always loudly invoked in behalf of anarchistic agitators." It chided the professors for "preaching the doctrine of laziness" and invited them to establish their own university, "provide the funds, erect the buildings, lay out the campus, and then make a requisition on the padded cells of Bedlam for their teaching staff."[17]

Even within the academy some observers warned about the dangers of allowing faculty, in the name of academic freedom, to "get beyond the easy depths of their own special academic vested interests" and remarked "how ill-fitted the average faculty member is to form really intelligent questions about large educational issues."[18]

Despite decades of ongoing controversy, the principles of academic freedom are today securely established within the functions and structures of the higher-education industry, including, as we shall see, in the for-profit sector. Faculty are free to conduct research and publish their results without institutional censure or any undue political or ideological constraints. Federal and state governments place no limitations on academic freedom. The AAUP, academic freedom's watchdog, is actually presented with relatively few cases involving institutional violation of academic freedom.[19]

Exactly what do we mean by *academic freedom?* Today, the answer is usually something like "the freedom to pursue the truth wherever it leads," or "the freedom to discuss any topic in the classroom," or "the freedom to conduct scholarly inquiry into any topic." The idea is to be free to do these things without the fear of being sanctioned or punished or prevented from doing them in any way by administrators, trustees, government agents, or anyone else. But all of this is tricky ground. We know from history that serious harm can be done in the name of pursuing the truth, such as the "truth" of Marxist nationalism under Stalin or the "truth" of National Socialism under Hitler.

The meaning of academic freedom comes more clearly into focus when we go back to the 1940 Statement of Principles on Academic Freedom and Tenure, published jointly by the AAUP and the Association of American Colleges. The 1940 statement grants several freedoms to faculty members, but to each freedom it attaches certain caveats and responsibilities. It allows, for example, that faculty should be free to do research and publish the results "subject to the adequate performance of their other academic duties." In the classroom, they should be free "in discussing their subject, but they should be careful not to introduce controversial matter which has no relation to their subject." As representatives of the academy, they should be free to write and speak as citizens, "but their special position requires special obligations." Most important, they "should at all times be accurate, should exercise appropriate restraint, [and] should show respect for the opinions of others."[20]

These statements seem eminently reasonable, and virtually all college-level teachers do, in fact, enjoy these freedoms. But what about the academic freedom of faculty in the for-profit universities?

Academic Freedom in the For-Profit Sector

The heyday of academic freedom in the United States was probably the twenty years between 1960 and 1980. McCarthyism was just a bad memory, and the extreme political correctness required today in the use of language had not yet been invented. During that period the college classroom was, like the Internet in the 1990s, the great frontier and bastion of freedom of expression. "You could use the F word," says one of my DeVry colleagues who spent many years in traditional universities. "You could champion pornography, Marxism, bestiality, or whatever, and use words like *nigger* and say *he* when you meant *he or she*." As a professor, when you walked into the classroom and closed the door, you were in a sacred space where any use of language and nearly any form of self-expression were allowed.

Today, the classroom is not so free. The excesses of political correctness and fear of offending others have brought about fundamental changes in the use of language in the classroom. If you want to champion bestiality, you had better couch it as a rhetorical stance, under the guise of an argument for argument's sake. Only then, in most instances, is it still protected under academic freedom. The center of gravity shifts even further in the for-profit sector, where if you want to champion bestiality, you had better do it on your own time and rather quietly, if at all.

In the for-profit environment faculty generally have one boss, their academic dean, who is usually referred to as the academic manager. He or she is responsible for supervising the work of the faculty. In contrast, in a traditional university, through an elaborate system of shared governance, the faculty are self-managing, and their work is largely unsupervised. A dean at a traditional university would seldom conceive of him- or herself primarily as one who supervises the faculty. Indeed, one way of characterizing the bottom-line intent of academic freedom is to say that faculty are protected from being supervised by anyone. In the monastic college tradition academic communities were self-governing, and members of the community lived by rules and discipline enforced by the community. The modern university, however, has lost this communal identity,[21] and one result is that the work of the faculty is unsupervised.*

All this shifts in the for-profit environment, where, for example, aca-

---

*Some readers may consider peer review to be a form of supervision. Having lived and worked in the for-profit academic environment, I do not share this view. Supervision in the for-profits is conducted by one's bosses, not by one's peers.

demic credentials are only one aspect of the desired job qualifications for members of the faculty. Equally important is having substantial professional experience in the field, and this is true for many of the general-education as well as the technical faculty. Argosy Education's faculty who teach in the doctoral programs in clinical psychology, whether on a full-time or an adjunct basis, are required to have substantial and ongoing clinical experience in the field. Training and practice in these clinical settings involves a significant amount of supervision, so that one's work is closely scrutinized by other persons in positions of authority. Such experience not only pays off in the classroom, where students are hungry to learn from someone who has been there, but also provides a context in which one understands and accepts the fact that one's work as a professor will be supervised.

The use of the word *supervised* is not meant to imply that deans stand by with a stopwatch and clipboard. However, for-profit deans visit the classrooms regularly and provide faculty with written observations, which are then discussed. Regular classroom observations by deans are considered neither unusual nor problematic; they are simply part of the culture. Student-feedback forms are used in every class section every semester, and while they are viewed with the same healthy skepticism found in traditional institutions, the results are reviewed by the deans and become part of the faculty member's annual performance review. Grade distributions and student-retention data are also reviewed each semester. Wide deviations from the norm for similar courses are discussed with the faculty member, and changes are expected as a result.

The reality of the for-profit environment is that everyone's work is supervised by someone else. To some extent, this results in less independence for faculty than in traditional academic cultures. Add to that the strong emphasis on serving the customers found in the for-profits, and it may seem that faculty in these institutions have somewhat less academic freedom than those in the traditional sector. Perhaps the best way to address this question is to return to the AAUP's 1940 statement, which defines *academic freedom* in three components: (1) the freedom to do research and publish the results; (2) the freedom to discuss subject matter in the classroom; and (3) the freedom to write and speak as citizens.

The first of these three is clearly available to faculty in the for-profits, even though scholarly activity is not a dominant part of the educational mission of these institutions. For example, the *Academic Policy Manual* at DeVry includes the following statement in the section on academic freedom:

> DeVry supports the right of its faculty and staff to engage in scholarly and creative activities, to make pubic presentations, and to present issues openly in the classroom. DeVry encourages its faculty and other employees to develop themselves professionally through various means, which may include writing for publication, making presentations, designing inventions and technical improvements, and maintaining contact and communication with educational and professional groups in their fields.[22]

Faculty at DeVry and the other for-profits are not required to obtain any special legal or other approvals before publishing their scholarly and creative work.

Similarly, skipping for a moment to the third area of academic freedom, the freedom to write and speak as citizens appears to be fully available to faculty at the for-profits. Indeed, this freedom is guaranteed constitutionally by the Bill of Rights and the First Amendment. There is no evidence that for-profit universities have acted in any way to inhibit these rights.

The second freedom, however, pertaining to freedom of speech in the classroom, is where things get more interesting. The DeVry *Academic Policy Manual* contains the following statement:

> In the classroom, both the discussion of issues and the use of written or visual materials must be conducted in an impartial spirit and must be accompanied by tolerance for differing views and by discretion regarding the sensibilities of students and others. *DeVry reserves the right to establish the educational mission and the goals of the curriculum, and requires faculty to address the course terminal objectives which define the scope and level of their courses* (emphasis added).[23]

The stipulation here is that faculty are required to teach the subject matter they have been assigned. They are not free to significantly alter the basic goals and objectives of the course. There probably is an inherent element of lost freedom in this requirement since the faculty do not develop these goals and objectives as free agents. However, in focus groups of faculty at DeVry in which academic freedom was discussed, almost all faculty said that felt they had sufficient academic freedom. The one constraint some of them feel is that they have little time to exercise their academic freedom outside the classroom. Heavy teaching loads and year-round teaching schedules leave little time for ongoing scholarly pursuits, and this has the net effect of limiting their sense of academic freedom.

There is another, more substantial influence on what goes on in the for-profit classroom. A faculty member's freedom of expression is tempered by one formidable consideration: the students. Because students are the paying customers, their opinions about what goes on in the classroom are usually taken at face value, or something close to it. If students perceive a problem with teaching quality, or text materials, or grading, this is considered important feedback. The faculty are there to serve the students, not the other way around. It is ultimately the students who set the standard for what is appropriate and acceptable in terms of freedom of expression. This philosophy is grounded in the standard customer-service orientation of any successful for-profit venture, and it is part of the culture of successful for-profit institutions of higher education. If a student in a proprietary institution is offended by a faculty member's use of language, for example, and complains to the dean that the faculty member curses while lecturing, chances are that the faculty member will be asked modify his language. His supervisor will require it.

Academic Freedom of Students

In effect, the balance of power in the for-profits represents a shift away from the faculty and toward the students, who are not just treated like customers, they *are* the customers. This shift in power impacts the nature of the relationship between students and faculty, and it transfers to the students a share of the academic freedom typically held exclusively by the faculty in more traditional environments. Indeed, it is probably fair to say that students in the for-profits have more power than they do in traditional academic institutions, while faculty have less. This shift in the balance of power raises concerns about adequate safeguards against giving away grades and watering down rigor for the sake of creating happy customers. It also begs the question whether faculty in the for-profits have sufficient academic freedom. Both of these issues—academic rigor and academic freedom—are at the heart of the cultural distinction between the for-profit university and traditional academic institutions.

The corporate emphasis on student retention and completion rates in the for-profits does indeed put pressure on the faculty. Failure rates and student attrition are tracked weekly for all courses. It is assumed that different sections of the same course should have reasonably similar distributions of grades, failures, and student attrition. Deviations from the norm are considered red flags, especially if they persist over several semesters. Courses with high attrition are called "killer courses," and the faculty who teach them are sometimes called "killer faculty." Deans are asked to look into these situations and discuss them with the faculty member. In some cases, higher failure rates and higher attrition can be traced back to lower student scores on admissions and placement tests. Just as frequently, the problem is related to the attitude and expectations of the faculty member, and the dean will explore these is some detail. All of this can be avoided, of course, if the faculty member's failure rates and attrition rates are low. While there is no explicit mandate to go easy on students or to be an easy grader, there is nonetheless some pressure to do so. This is where some would say that academic freedom and academic rigor are being compromised.

On my campus, I was curious to see whether the pressure to be an easy grader was reflected in the distribution of grades awarded each semester. Over the past several semesters, a typical distribution of final grades has been as follows:

	A	B	C	D	F	W or I
Percent	33	27	16	6	6	11
Number	4,179	3,349	2,010	791	745	1,394

These figures show that 60 percent of the final grades awarded were As and Bs, while only 12 percent were Ds and Fs. While clearly skewed toward the high end, this distribution is actually not out of line with the inflated grading going on all across American higher education, even at "rigorous" universities. At Princeton, for example, a study showed that between 1992 and 1997, 83 percent of the grades awarded were As and Bs. During the 1980s the percentage of As awarded at Yale never fell below 40 percent. At Stanford, Columbia, Dartmouth, Harvard, and the University of Pennsylvania about 40 percent of the grades awarded are As.[24] Even at less prestigious schools, such as Rider University, a medium-sized, private institution with moderate admission standards, more than 50 percent of all final grades are As and Bs.[25] Arthur Levine's national study of grading patterns showed that between 1969 and 1993 the percentage of Cs awarded fell from 25 percent to 9 percent, while the percentage of As rose from 7 percent to 26 percent.[26] The ubiquity of grade inflation, then, makes it difficult to draw any firm conclusions about the possibility of increased pressure to give good grades at for-profit universities.

"The pressure to go easy on students," says one veteran for-profit professor, "is not so much on giving away grades as on giving students many opportunities to redo, revise, re-think, make-up, and re-take. Students are always redoing lab experiments and rewriting essays, until they get it right." This "try again" philosophy is also part of the academic culture of the for-profits, where a pedagogy that encourages repetition and reinforcement is favored.

Of course, good students, especially the older students that the for-profits tend to attract, are demanding customers who often expect rigor in the classroom and feel cheated if they don't get it. Most have attended other colleges and are highly motivated to learn the skills and gain the knowledge needed to advance their careers. They usually know a well-designed course, substantive subject matter, and good teaching when they see it. In no small way, the primary safeguard against the lack of rigor in for-profit colleges is probably the demands of students themselves.

Student Life in the For-Profits

The publicly held for-profit universities cater almost exclusively to commuter students. There are no organized sports teams, no student-center buildings, and very limited if any organized recreational activities for students. The focus is on classroom instruction and lab work. Interestingly, most students in the for-profits rate the student-life aspects of their experience as fully meeting their needs, probably in part because they are not seeking activities that do not relate to their educational goals.

DeVry students, for example, annually participate in the national Noel-Levitz Student Satisfaction Inventory.[27] Results have consistently shown that DeVry students do not find the campus climate lacking, despite the absence of programs and activities one might normally associate with college life. In fact, DeVry students rate their "campus climate" (a scale comprising 17 items on the questionnaire) as highly as students on traditional campuses rate theirs, and they rate "campus life" (a scale of 15 items) higher than the national average of students rate theirs.

Student clubs and organizations are somewhat limited but generally active. Most campuses have an active student government association, but its role is limited compared with those on traditional campuses. Students tend not to be represented on faculty and administrative committees. For-profit students are not politically active on their campuses, presumably because such activity requires more time than they have and is seen as being unrelated to their educational objectives. Interestingly, none of the campuses of the large for-profits I visited have a student newspaper. Several do have a student literary magazine.

While extracurricular and recreational activities are purposely limited at for-profits, student advising is fully addressed. Academic advising, career counseling, and personal counseling are emphasized. From a purely business standpoint, these activities are seen as contributing to the bottom line through improved student retention, completion, and placement rates. Student advising is a regular part of faculty responsibilities, and most campuses also have a staff of full-time professional advisers for first-year students as well as counselors who help students deal with personal problems. Serious cases are referred to local community agencies and independent professional counselors. Peer advising and tutoring are also popular at the for-profits. Students are encouraged to form study groups, and they are often required to do so as part of the course design. Career-advising and job-placement services are especially strong since high placement rates are an important strength of these institutions, as we saw in chapter 4.

Attendance policies are stringent, in part because the for-profits are under closer scrutiny than non-profits to account for the disbursement of student-aid dollars. Part of this accountability involves verifying the last date of attendance for each student who discontinues study. At DeVry, attendance is taken at every class meeting. Students who miss five days of classes in a semester are subject to dismissal from the institution and must go through an appeal process to gain readmission. Aside from the financial-aid-disbursement issue, the strict attendance policy provides students with a motivation to be disciplined about their use of time. Most students respond dutifully to the structure created by the policy of required attendance.

For-profit students are serious about their studies. Their goal is to "get in, get out, and get a job," and they are not particularly concerned about their collegiate social life, "finding themselves," or studying abroad. They seek a no-nonsense academic experience tied to a practical outcome.

6

Lessons from the For-Profit Side

The beat poet Allen Ginsberg visited my campus in the fall of 1969, when I was an undergraduate English major at a large state university in the Midwest. He spoke in a kind of prose-poem about the purpose of American universities, characterizing them as giant warehouses designed to occupy the time of young people that society did not know what else to do with. A proper college education, he suggested, was simply a way of efficiently housing people who were too young to be adults and too old to be children. Most of the assembled students, myself included, identified strongly with Ginsberg's straightforward explanation of our own experience.

The giant-warehouse metaphor may still work in some of the large, state university systems, but in general it no longer describes reality. For one thing, the demographics have radically changed. Half of the college students in America are adults, and only about 7 percent are 18- to 22-year-olds living on campus and pursuing liberal arts degrees.[1] Perhaps even more dramatic, it has become increasingly common to tie the outcome of a college education to the economic earning power of graduates, and that is how the payoff is measured in many studies (more on this below). The earning power of graduates is in turn tied to regional and national economic health. The National Center for Education Statistics now tracks the relationship between national productivity, the educational attainment of individuals, and individual earning power, which it uses to demonstrate the tangible benefits of investing in education to the economic well-being of the nation.[2] One recent NCES report asserts that improvements in worker productivity in the United States are the result of increases in educational attainment and that the "best available measure of a worker's productivity is that worker's wages."[3]

The focused educational missions and values of the for-profit providers fit harmoniously into this conversation about the relationship between educational attainment, the earning power of graduates, and national productivity. These institutions thrive on providing an efficient and cost-effective route to a degree and job placement in a high-demand field at a good salary. This, in essence, is what they do as educational providers. Allen Ginsberg might have described it as mass assembly-line job training tied to the needs of the market. A small but growing proportion of students (ca. 400,000 in 2000) and, to a lesser extent, faculty (ca. 30,000 full-time faculty in 2000) are choosing to study and teach in these pragmatic, applications-oriented colleges and universities.[4]

The rise of the for-profit model in higher education, and in particular the growth of the large, publicly traded corporations that offer accredited degree programs at the associate's, baccalaureate, master's, and even doctoral levels, will continue to have a profound influence on the higher-education industry in America. Having examined the history, growth, organizational culture, and financing of for-profit universities in previous chapters, I seek to accomplish two primary goals in this final chapter. The first is to frame the for-profit model within the larger context of the continuing development of higher education in general and to identify how for-profit institutions are influencing our evolving understanding of what constitutes a college education. My second goal is to identify some of the lessons that traditional higher-education institutions may learn from the reemergence and growth of the for-profit providers. By understanding what seems to be working well in the for-profit model, in particular by observing how the for-profits are addressing needs that are not being met by some traditional colleges and universities, traditional institutions may be able to more clearly understand and articulate their own values and purposes.

To begin, it is useful to identify some of the ways in which the lines are blurring between for-profit and non-profit institutions.

Blurring of the Lines

At the level of the classroom, as related in chapter 5, the for-profit and non-profit sectors are indistinguishable. The better for-profits, such as Strayer University, in the Washington-Baltimore corridor, Education Management Corporation, which owns and operates the art institutes, and Argosy Education Group, which offers doctoral programs through the ten campuses of the American Schools of Psychology and the University of Sarasota, are legitimate and viable academic institutions. Meanwhile, growing numbers of well-known non-profit universities are adapting their organizational structure to create for-profit arms, focused on adult continuing education and venture-capital formation. This trend, which is worth watching and perhaps worth emulating, is discussed in greater detail below. Clearly, the growing number of new for-profit ventures within non-profit universities are indicators that the terms *for-profit* and *non-profit* are becoming less meaningful in making distinctions among institutions of all types and at all levels of quality. This blurring of the lines began to escalate during the economic boom of the 1990s, when major improvements in educational quality and significant new growth occurred in the for-profit sector, while at the same time the traditional model of higher education was being questioned from within and criticized from without for its inefficiency, unresponsiveness, and resistance to change.

As a result of this blurring of the lines, the higher-education institutional landscape is changing significantly. College students of all ages and at all degree levels now have a broader menu of options to choose from in pursuing their educational goals. Faculty members too have a new set of career options to consider, a set of options that replaces the tenure track with stock options, sidesteps the scholarly-productivity game altogether, and provides them with clearly defined institutional roles. Further, the stigma associated with being "proprietary" is slowly disappearing. Michael Markovitz, who founded and developed the highly successful Psy.D. program at Argosy (see chapter 2), says about the founding of the institution that "there was no real sense that it was more noble to be non-profit. The nobility lay in the execution of the idea."[5]

Still, one of the concerns within the traditional academy about the for-profit providers is whether they provide a legitimate college education or merely job training. Here again, however, the distinctions have blurred. The difference between what we call teaching and what we call training is not particularly clear except, perhaps, in the extreme. Cosmetology schools provide training, not education. Medical schools provide a combination of training and education, as do schools of law, engineering, art, and architecture, among others. Without question, good trainers engage in teaching and good teachers use training techniques. Training implies mastering skills through learning. As educators, we expect and we hope that teaching accomplishes something greater, something more like "opening minds." If someone's mind is opened while they are being taught, we might naturally want to attribute that to effective teaching (and perhaps to effective learning). If someone's mind is opened while they are getting trained, however, we might be reluctant to attribute that to effective training.

The question what constitutes a legitimate college education—what should be studied and learned and how it should be taught—is part of an evolving conversation that continues to be shaped by both traditional ideals and the pragmatic appetites of the market economy. Perhaps this has always been the case, especially in American higher education, which emulated but did not exactly copy the European university model and which could not ultimately survive in total isolation from the influences of the economic marketplace. Alongside the creation of the first classical colleges in the United States, as discussed in chapter 3, there were also thriving alternative, often subversive, and sometimes underground proprietary schools whose existence was sustained by needs unmet by the traditional model. Higher education in America, from the classical colleges to the mechanical arts schools, and from the land-grant universities to the correspondence schools, is the product of both tradition and the imperative of contemporary market demands.

Many traditional colleges have continued to emphasize the protection of tradition over the response to market demands. The for-profit providers pay homage to academic tradition, and indeed they must do so to gain regional association accreditation, but they place a higher value on meeting market demands. There is room for both of these purveyors of higher education, and although the distinction between them is blurring, both approaches can be carried out with integrity.

Measuring Value by the Earning Power of Graduates

Throughout this book I have argued that what the for-profits do exceptionally well is respond to the marketplace. In the case of freshmen students (students in their first year of study at the college level), national survey data indicate that the for-profits provide what many of these customers say they want. The annual survey of freshmen conducted by the Higher Education Research Institute at UCLA, now in its thirty-fifth year, has tracked the increasing level of disengagement with traditional academics and the emerging dominance of the goal of financial well-being on the part of college freshmen.[6] The most recent survey, released in January 2000, asked a sample of 261,217 students to rank order a list of 13 reasons they considered very important in deciding to go to college. At the top of the list was the reason "to be able to get a better job" (72% of respondents), followed by "to get training for a specific career" (72%). Out of 20 goals they hoped to achieve by going to college, "being very well off financially" topped the list (73.4%), well in front of the old standard, "developing a meaningful philosophy of life" (39.7%).

Again, these survey findings reflect the attitudes of college freshman and do not necessarily reflect the values of institutions of higher education. It may be argued, for instance, that even where employability is the explicit goal of the student, and even of the curriculum, students may be helped to develop a meaningful philosophy of life whether or not they consider it a priority. And yet it seems clear that students' attitudes toward and expectations of their college education are strongly oriented to career advancement and economic return.

Such attitudes and expectations have perhaps become so common among college students today that they are taken for granted by the higher-education community. In fact, the primary yardstick for assessing the value of an institution's undergraduate degrees has evolved to become a matter of the earning power of graduates. For example, several studies have confirmed that the high price of a degree from an Ivy League university does indeed result in a successful career launch and high-paying employment.[7] One such study, released late in 1999 by the National Bureau of Economic Research, compared the value of a degree from a highly selective institution, such as Yale or Bryn Mawr, with the value of a degree from a less prestigious institution, such as Denison or Tulane. The only variable used in this study to assess the value of the degrees was the average earned income of the graduates.[8] Whether these graduates developed a meaningful philosophy of life was not even considered.

People expect educational success to bring economic success. Roseann Runte, president of Victoria University in Toronto, has pointed out that even the 1996 report of the International Commission on Education for the Twenty-first Century of the United Nations Educational, Scientific, and Cultural Organization, entitled *Learning: The Treasure Within,* is really not about the "treasure within" at all, but about how education generates financial wealth for individuals and nations.[9] Education provides an opportunity for an improved quality of life, and the easiest way to measure that in a materialistic society is in the practical realm of economic return.

That the value of a college degree is assessed on the basis of how much money graduates earn and that such assessments are regularly conducted by researchers both inside and outside academia would seem to strongly support the conclusion that higher education in the United States is essentially becoming a process of providing credentials, whose value is measured in terms of economic return. On that particular score the for-profits rank highly, as do the elite, highly selective institutions.

Two Guardians of Quality and Integrity

Two distinct guardians of institutional quality and integrity are at work in the higher-education industry. One is the accreditation process. In simple terms, accreditation verifies that a "proper college education," consistent with the institution's mission and meeting or exceeding thresholds of approved standards of education quality, is attainable at an institution. The accreditation process is not perfect, but the vast majority of institutions appear to find it helpful in addressing problems and improving overall quality.

The for-profit providers treat accreditation as a business objective. They have demonstrated that meeting accreditation standards is essentially the direct result of properly allocating resources. The standards themselves, whether pertaining to faculty credentials or to the adequacy of the library, are surrogate measures of a quality education, but they do not guarantee quality. Within the universe of accredited colleges and universities there is obviously wide variability of institutional quality, in both the non-profit and for-profit sectors.

Surely it makes sense that all educational institutions, whether organized on a for-profit or a non-profit basis, should meet the same standards for accreditation. Historically, however, this has not been the case, and several states and regions still have on their books a different, often more stringent set of standards for the for-profit schools. "The problem with accreditation," says Jorge de Alva of Phoenix, "is that institutions like the University of Phoenix, because they are owned by a for-profit company, are held to a different set of regulations."[10] State licensing standards, too, often hold proprietary institutions to different standards, as in the case of New Jersey, which has separate rules for licensing proprietary institutions and limits the duration of the license to five years (as opposed to a one-time license for non-profit colleges and universities).

Judith Eaton, president of the Council for Higher Education Accreditation, notes that regional accreditation is "one of the oldest and most frequently used forms of institutional quality assurance in the United States."[11] As the regional associations rise to the challenge of the changing face of higher education, especially the advancements in distance learning and the rapid growth of for-profit institutions and for-profit arms of non-profit institutions, they are revisiting the core academic values that have long guided the regional association accreditation standards. Eaton summarizes these core academic values as follows:

- Institutional autonomy
- Collegiality and shared governance
- The intellectual and academic authority of the faculty

- The degree (whether associate's, baccalaureate, professional, master's, or doctorate)
- General education
- Site-based education and a community of learning

Regional association accreditation, says Eaton, exists to protect these core values. "Evidence of a lack of institutional commitment to even one of these values," she asserts, "is cause for sanctions, from additional scrutiny of an institution to withdrawal of accreditation."[12] What must be acknowledged is that for-profit providers operate under a different hierarchy of values, especially as they pertain to the second and third values listed above. As discussed in chapters 1 and 5, shared governance does not accurately describe how the for-profit universities profiled in this book handle the decision-making process. While there is faculty participation in some decisions, there is none in others. For example, the faculty at DeVry, Strayer, Education Management, and others do not decide which degree programs are offered by their campuses, and often they do not even participate in discussions on this topic. In addition, the intellectual and academic authority of the faculty, by which Eaton means responsibility for the curriculum, course content, and academic standards for evaluating student performance, differs significantly in the for-profit environment. In my experience, although the faculty in the for-profits have some influence over these areas, they do not have final authority over the curriculum, course content, or academic standards.

The regional associations are currently in the process of reexamining both the standards for accreditation and the processes used to assess institutional compliance with them. It is fair to say that these standards are both descriptive and prescriptive. That is, to some extent the standards are derived from descriptions of "good" institutions and are then used as a prescriptive base for all institutions. The process of making the standards prescriptive inevitably encounters different descriptive possibilities. The for-profits raise the specter that "good" institutions should be responsible stewards of financial, human, and physical resources, held accountable for their efficient and effective use. Thus, questions of institutional integrity would be modified to encompass a different set of values. The art and science of accreditation depends on achieving a balance between descriptive and prescriptive realities. At its best, the process remains open in both the application of existing standards and the modification of existing standards in response to other demonstrations of institutional quality and integrity.

The other guardian of institutional quality and integrity is the free-market economy itself. At its best, the marketplace functions as a system of checks and balances in which good products and services are sustained by the buying public, while poor products and services eventually lose their markets to better competitors. Products and services that are responsive to the needs and demands of the market are consumed, and those that are not responsive are not consumed.

In the simplest of terms, *marketplace* in this context refers to the relationship between the demands that exist for certain kinds of higher education and the response of institutions to address these demands as measured by enrollments. In other words, the marketplace is a point of exchange between providers and consumers of higher education. For example, the fact that 100,000 adult students have enrolled at the University of Phoenix, when they obviously had many other choices of educational providers, indicates that the marketplace is confirming that what Phoenix is offering addresses the needs and demands of certain consumers. Whether Phoenix's success is a fluke, a matter of watered-down standards, or a case of duping the unsuspecting public is not readily revealed by this information alone.

Indeed, as a guardian of institutional integrity and quality, the marketplace is limited in terms of what it reveals about an institution and how it functions to improve quality. The market alone can not determine educational quality, particularly if educational quality is defined in terms of fulfilling the needs of society, for the market is entirely attuned to current demands and does not necessarily account for the larger needs of society. Perhaps there are inevitable tensions between individual perceptions of need, such as one's economic earning power, and the needs of human community and society. Consequently, it may be reasonable to assume that some institutions must swim upstream against the current tide of the marketplace in order to preserve values that extend beyond such goals as improving individual economic earning power. The consumer marketplace itself is somewhat valueless; it reflects whatever values consumers themselves bring to the exchange.

What the marketplace does reveal, however, is useful in terms of assessing how well an institution is attuned to current market demands, as well as how effectively the institution meets the current expectations of educational consumers. In higher education as in other service industries, such as health care and financial services, consumer-market responsiveness is an increasingly important aspect of institutional effectiveness. The rise of the for-profit providers has ushered in a new level of marketplace accountability in higher education, and in my assessment, such accountability will be increasingly demanded of the majority of non-profit colleges and universities as well.

The Luxury of Inefficiency

One of the questions traditional educators sometimes ask me about the for-profit universities is, Where is their intellectual center? I am not always certain what they mean by this question, but the concern behind the question has to do with the apparent departure of the for-profits from the traditions of tenure, academic freedom, and shared governance.

In the traditional model, the intellectual center of the institution lies with the full-time faculty, who are entrusted with authority over the curriculum, instruction, and course content and who are granted considerable voice in all major decisions that affect institutional life. In this model, a large amounts of release time from classroom teaching— as much as one-third or one-half of the standard teaching load—is often defended on the basis of its direct and indirect contributions to the institution's mission and, more to the point, to the health of the institution's intellectual center. Certain forms of instructional inefficiency in the deployment of full-time faculty, such as team teaching and very small classes, are tolerated and even celebrated because it is believed that the "luxury of inefficiency," as Patricia McGuire, president of Trinity College, calls it, is an important investment in the intellectual foundation of the institution.[13]

As attractive as the concept may be, it is difficult to make a sensible case for the luxury of inefficiency for all of higher education. The benefits of being inefficient in the use of financial, human, and physical resources are not clear. The supposed outcomes have tended to be accepted on faith and not on the basis of outcomes measures. Despite the adoption of the language of "assessment of outcomes," there remains a considerable lack of measurement of and accountability for results within many universities. What is sometimes celebrated in the name of the luxury of inefficiency may simply be a form of organizational ineffectiveness.[14] Concerning the emphasis on faculty research in many colleges and universities, for example, Zachary Karabell, among others, has argued that the emphasis on faculty research all across academia has resulted in the duplication and triplication of the research already being carried out by faculty at the major research universities.[15] And while it is presumed that faculty research contributes to better classroom teaching, this has not been proven and may be true primarily for certain fields only at the graduate level of instruction.

In the classroom, it is presumed that smaller classes, of, say, fewer than 20 students, result in improved learning and better student performance, especially in such subjects as freshman composition. Having for many years taught freshman composition myself, I admit to clearly preferring a class of 20 to a class of 30, but I could not offer proof that improved learning and better student performance resulted from my smaller classes. There were simply too many other variables at play, such as the skill level of the collection of students in a particular class, the classroom dynamics among particular groups of students, and the variability of my own performance as a teacher on certain days and at certain times. The nondebatable and measurable difference between a freshman composition class of 30 and one of 20 was the amount of work I had to do, for reading 30 student papers unquestionably involves more work than does reading 20.

Not that the for-profit providers have very large classes; they do not. Even the standard-bearer of efficiency, the University of Phoenix, has an average class size in the teens and a student-to-faculty ratio of 18 to 1. Of course, these are primarily part-time faculty, and this brings us back to the question of the location of the institution's intellectual center.

Defining the Intellectual Center

In the for-profit model generally, the full-time faculty occupy the intellectual center of the institution just as they do in traditional universities. The students, who are generally older, working adults with families, also significantly contribute to this intellectual center, just as they do in traditional institutions. Unlike in traditional non-profit institutions, however, the authority of the faculty in for-profits over decisions that affect institutional life is more controlled. Without tenure and lacking many of the standard trappings of shared governance, such as faculty senates and promotion-and-tenure committees, the faculty in these institutions are deployed to teach, not to govern the institution.

At Educational Management, Argosy, Strayer, and DeVry the full-time faculty generally teach 50–70 percent of the credit hours taught during an academic year. Release time from teaching for curriculum development, professional development, and continuing education, as well as time off from teaching responsibilities during sabbatical leaves, is available to the full-time faculty who work in these for-profit providers.

At DeVry, for example, in addition to a paid sabbatical every five years, faculty have the option of banking extra teaching hours (usually by teaching an additional course in the evenings or on weekends) and then cashing them in for release time. In a typical academic year, release time from teaching responsibilities on my DeVry campus constitutes about 10 percent of the total full-time workload, or about 350 hours of release time out of a total workload of about 3,500 hours, which translates into the equivalent of eight full-time faculty positions released from teaching. About half of this release time is for sabbaticals, and the other half is for curriculum development and administrative responsibilities for department chairs. Faculty at DeVry are seldom released from teaching for research projects, except when those projects are related to the completion of a Ph.D. dissertation, in which case they may be released from 50–100 percent of their teaching load.

Based on my work in and study of the for-profit universities, I believe a strong argument could be made that the intellectual center at some of these for-profit campuses is at least as viable as that at many traditional institutions, even though the for-profits do not place as high a value on faculty research. This is certainly the case at Argosy's American Schools of Professional Psychology, where the faculty are required by contract to be on campus four days each week and are held accountable for the delivery of instruction and for the learning outcomes of the courses they teach, which they themselves develop. Instead of research and publication, Argosy's psychology faculty are actively involved in clinical practice, which clearly informs their teaching and shapes the curriculum. At the art institutes of Education Management the faculty are on campus five days a week and work closely together and with their students to build and maintain a strong sense of a community of artists. At the DeVry Institutes of Technology many faculty are deeply involved in ongoing discussions of pedagogy and student learning styles, especially in the areas of general education, which on my New Jersey campus comprises 50 percent of the coursework in each technical degree program. What is noteworthy about the full-time faculty in these institutions in terms of their contributions to the intellectual center is that they are present, on campus, four or five days each week.

But what about the intellectual center of an institution like the University of Phoenix, which employs part-time faculty almost exclusively? Can there be an intellectual center at an institution where nearly all the faculty are "adjuncts"? Jorge de Alva, Phoenix's president, recently addressed this question at a meeting of the Council for Higher Education Accreditation.[16] He drew an interesting distinction: "To me," he said, "the fundamental difference is not between full-time and part-time faculty, but rather between practitioner faculty and self-employed faculty." Phoenix does not refer to its faculty as "adjuncts" because they are not "adjunctive" but are rather the instructional centerpiece of the institution. A condition of employment as a faculty member at Phoenix is full-time engagement as a practitioner in the field being taught. Phoenix's founder and CEO, John Sperling, puts it this way: "If you don't do it by day, you can't teach it at night."[17]

De Alva, reflecting on his years as a tenured professor at Princeton and as the holder of an endowed chair at Berkeley, says: "The full-time faculty of many traditional institutions are essentially self-employed, independent agents, who are expected to advance their careers and bring acclaim to their institutions through scholarly publications, grants, fellowships, and prizes." Operating under such expectations, argues De Alva, these faculty are often absent from their campuses, absent from the classroom, and absent from direct involvement in governance, and they are therefore contributing not so much to the institution's intellectual center as to their own careers and to the advancement of knowledge in the disciplines. He suggests that Phoenix's faculty are actually more present and engaged than the full-time faculty at many traditional universities and therefore more able to contribute to the institution's intellectual center.

Whatever our conclusions about the intellectual center of the University of Phoenix (and the other for-profit providers), we must ask whether it matters at all to most undergraduate students. One suspects that it does not.

Learning from the For-Profits

"Now, and even more in the future, what goes on in the university is inseparable from who we are as a nation," writes Zachary Karabell in *What's College For?*[18] Karabell suggests convincingly that U.S. higher education is undergoing a revolution, "becoming mass education and in the process being radically democratized."[19] Access to higher education by students of all backgrounds and ability levels is one of the strengths of the U.S. system.

Surely another strength is the diversity of colleges and universities within the system itself, providing students with choices and options for pursuing their education. The diversity of institutional missions allows many institutions to excel in particular areas, whether basic scholarship in certain fields or serving the local community with associate's-degree programs. The for-profit providers represent another form of institutional and missional diversity, one that serves a useful purpose and contributes to the overall vitality and breadth of the higher-education industry.

In my involvement with for-profit institutions I have often thought about what the non-profits could learn from the for-profits. From the other side, it seems clear that the for-profits have taken cues from traditional institutions, for they have essentially taken the traditional model of higher education—students seated in the classroom and a professor up front—and subjected it to modern principles of operations management, cost accounting, financial management, and marketing. The result has been an efficient, cost-effective, alternative route to a college degree, albeit with a somewhat limited focus on pragmatic, applications-oriented instruction. In considering what traditional non-profit colleges and universities may learn from these successful for-profit institutions, four areas for change suggest themselves:

- Responding to market forces
- Adapting the organizational structure
- Redefining shared governance
- Developing a strong customer orientation

RESPONDING TO MARKET FORCES

Reflecting on the remarkable growth of higher education in the United States and the apparent preeminence of the U.S. university system worldwide, some observers have suggested that while the traditional university has been slow to change, it has also demonstrated a remarkable ability to adapt and respond.[20] Others have faulted the academy for its inherent resistance to change.[21] Of course, change is inevitable, whether in the demography of students, the economy, or the uses of technology, and the impact of change is variable in terms of its pace and scope. But as I have argued and illustrated throughout this book, in the area of market responsiveness many traditional colleges and universities have been resistant to change, responding slowly and adapting reluctantly. This becomes especially apparent when one looks at how quickly and effectively some of the for-profit education companies have responded to change, particularly regarding curriculum development, new program offerings, alternative instructional delivery, and academic decision making. Having lived and worked in both environments, I have found the contrast striking.

Perhaps some traditional non-profit institutions have resisted change out of a sense of mission to protect values that are assumed to be essential to human society. Some may have been less concerned about the need for change in areas other than those stemming from scholarly advancements in the academic disciplines themselves. Others have simply paid little attention to the need for change, suffering from what William Tierney calls "organization attention deficit disorder."[22] Many simply lack a mechanism for addressing change. At one liberal arts college where I helped to develop a strategic plan, enrollments in the humanities had declined steadily for ten years and then remained low, while the scope of the humanities curriculum and the size of the humanities faculty had remained unchanged. Throughout most of its history, this college had geared itself to deal with growth and expansion, but there was no blueprint for how to cut back or significantly reallocate resources other than a cumbersome and unworkable layoff provision in the collective-bargaining agreement. The prevailing thinking expressed in faculty meetings was that enrollments were always cyclical and that the pendulum would swing back to the humanities in due time. Now, 18 years into the slump, enrollments in the humanities have still not rebounded.

"The university's tremendous inertia is the result of a long-standing, well-established system," write Patricia Gumport and Marc Chun, of Stanford University, in their analysis of higher education's resistance to technological change. "The scientific revolution took place for the most part outside of academe, and many academics shunned the industrial revolution."[23] As long as social, economic, and technological change was incremental and evolutionary, the traditional university's complex decision-making structure was not a fatal flaw in responding to market forces. However, as Scott Cowen, president of Tulane University, has suggested, social, economic, and technological change today is discontinuous and revolutionary, and in the face of this new reality the traditional decision-making process of the university "defies the logic of what you would expect of an effective organization."[24]

Aside from the 110 to 120 major research universities and an equal number of premier liberal arts colleges, by far the majority of American colleges and universities today are in the business of educating the work force.[25] In order to educate the work force, institutions must be in touch with the needs of the workplace, and the workplace is undergoing profound and constant transformation.[26] One way to document this transformation is to consider how long it now takes new products and services to reach a 25 percent market share. For example, it took an estimated 46 years for household electricity to achieve a 25 percent market-share penetration. The telephone took 35 years to penetrate 25 percent of its potential market, and the VCR, 34 years. The personal computer, however, took only 15 years, the cellular telephone, 13 years, and the Internet, 7 years.[27] These increasingly rapid rates of market penetration have not occurred in isolation but have been accompanied by changes in the education and training needs of many large industries and of the work force generally.

For these reasons, the majority of higher-education institutions must become more responsive to the market forces that impact the education and training needs of the students they serve. To do otherwise, warns Michael McPherson, president of Macalester College, "would leave us with not only greatly diminished resources, but with a greatly diminished voice in society and little basis beyond our own self-certainty for confidence in the effectiveness and value of what we do."[28] The question and the challenge is not whether to become more responsive but how to do so in the face of a tradition of resistance, a history of inertia, and a system of decision making that inhibits quick decisions and rapid response to change.

ADAPTING THE ORGANIZATIONAL STRUCTURE

One of the more fascinating developments in higher education at the turn of the twenty-first century is the creation of for-profit arms in several universities, including Columbia, Cornell, Stanford, New York University, and the University of Maryland, with others soon to follow. As noted earlier, this is a trend worth watching and perhaps emulating, especially for those institutions that have strong "brand" reputations in the markets they serve. "Branding will become increasingly important in the education industry," say industry analysts at Merrill Lynch, "just as it has become a prominent means of building companies in other industries." A strong brand identity is not limited to highly prestigious institutions, according to these analysts, who suggest that "there is opportunity for education brands to be built through inclusiveness and accessibility (as opposed to exclusiveness and inaccessibility) when coupled with high quality programs that have a consistent, positive impact on education achievement."[29]

Why, one might ask, would a non-profit university want to establish a for-profit venture—which would not qualify for tax-exempt status—as part of its operations? The answer is twofold and further attests to the blurring of the lines between non-profit and for-profit institutions.[30] First, these for-profit arms provide access to private investment capital, which, as we saw in chapter 4, functions as a kind of endowment in for-profit institutions. Universities with international brand identity, as well as institutions with strong regional or even local presence, are beginning to realize that their names and reputations can be used to attract potentially large sums of investment capital. If they are successful—it is a bit too soon to tell—they will have found a way to attract another form of "donated" income, through the investment of money from both individuals and corporations.

Second, there is relatively little financial risk involved in setting up these ventures. Even if they fail, the university itself will not go bankrupt or suffer financial exigency; it will simply continue to rely on its main business. (This is not true, of course, for the for-profit universities, whose main business is dependent upon private investment capital and sustained profitability and which are at considerable risk if either is lost.) These for-profit ventures are carefully structured to be located at arm's length from the university itself, so that the institution's core academic identity and culture are protected. In a sense, they offer an opportunity to participate in the for-profit game without the full measure of the for-profit risks.

From my own experience on the for-profit side, I would suggest that many colleges and universities should consider the benefits of establishing a for-profit venture as part of their total institutional structure. I recently gave such advice to a colleague who is provost at a small church-related college that is struggling to break free of living hand to mouth financially. Despite renewed efforts, fund-raising to increase the size of the institution's endowment was unsuccessful. This particular college has a strong entrepreneurial tradition, and twenty years ago it was among the first institutions in its metropolitan region to aggressively develop continuing-education programs for adult students. As an outsider looking in, I see the creation of a for-profit arm as having the potential to rekindle and channel this institution's entrepreneurial spirit and, in a sense, to allow it to give itself permission to be a more aggressive competitor in the market for continuing education for adults. College officials are now considering restructuring the continuing-education unit and reorganizing it as a for-profit entity.

Establishing a for-profit venture makes it possible for non-profit institutions to realize the best of both worlds: the tax advantages and fund-raising opportunities of a non-profit organization along with the capital-investment options and operating efficiencies of a for-profit corporation. They can do so without causing harm to their mission or their academic culture. The risks are minimal, and the potential financial rewards are substantial.

REDEFINING SHARED GOVERNANCE

Despite its appeal to traditional academic sensibilities (including my own), the concept of shared governance has evolved into a system of decision making that is unworkable on many campuses. For presidents, provosts, and deans, shared governance reduces leadership to making compromises and finding the "middle ground" in order to appease the loudest and offend the fewest. In practice, shared governance actually makes decision making a delusion altogether, says Daniel Julius, director of the Center for Strategic Leadership at the University of San Francisco.[31]

A new model is needed. The lesson of the for-profits is that a reasonable level of participation and inclusiveness can coexist within a more traditional management structure, in which authority for making decisions is granted to those in leadership positions. In working with faculty at DeVry, I see that less reliance on shared governance does not necessarily result in the destruction of academic culture; many faculty actually feel relieved to be freed from excessive participation in governance so that they can focus on their work as professors. There have also been times when I have felt that DeVry and perhaps other for-profits may have swung too far in the other direction, where the bosses wield power and sometimes fail to include the faculty sufficiently in decisions to which they could make important contributions, such as those involving curricula. I do not believe the for-profit providers have found the perfect solution to the problem of shared governance, but they have demonstrated that a more traditional management culture can work in an academic institution.

Perhaps every institution needs to find its own center of gravity in these matters. I am convinced that shared governance needs to be redefined to allow those in positions of authority to make decisions that are timely and responsive and to break free from what Daniel Julius describes as the political power struggle in which "decisions go round and round in circles, and the best one can hope for in the political battle is a temporary win."[32]

DEVELOPING A STRONG CUSTOMER ORIENTATION

The strong customer-service orientation of the for-profit colleges and universities profiled in this book is one of the reasons a growing population of students is choosing them in pursuit of higher education. As I have argued, treating students like customers does not mean that they cease to be students as well, or that the institution must give in to all their preferences, or that faculty must give away good grades for the sake of happy customers. It simply means that the institution becomes more responsive to its students and makes serving them effectively the highest priority. Failing to do so, I believe, will result in students' taking their business elsewhere.

Many students today respond well to a more professional, business-like relationship with their educational provider. For a growing number of students, attending a for-profit college has not only become a viable option; quite possibly it has also become "cool." My first hint that attending a for-profit college like DeVry might be considered "cool" among some students when I overheard a conversation between two freshmen on my own campus. One said that he had considered going to a nearby state university, and the other responded, "No way—DeVry is so much cooler than that." While I do not know exactly what this student meant by "cool," I know that it was a positive statement about his relationship with DeVry. My own perception of DeVry, against a lifetime spent in higher education, is of an educational provider that is utilitarian, practical, and no-frills, but responsive to its students. All good stuff, but not cool. Evergreen is cool, Warren Wilson is cool, Oberlin is cool—but DeVry? Perhaps many students do indeed consider these alternative providers as cool in part because they are treated like customers.

What Is a Proper College Education?

Any serious inquiry into the changing face of American higher education ultimately leads to the question what constitutes a proper college education. This question is a decidedly complex one.[33] Its answer inevitably depends on how one answers larger questions concerning epistemology, ontology, and the relationship between education and the greater social good. What can be known? How can it be known? What is the nature of the human knower? What is the purpose of knowledge? What is the meaning of human existence? What is the relationship between individual persons and democratic society? Answers to these kinds of fundamental questions implicitly or explicitly inform every attempt to define what constitutes a proper college education. Is it any surprise, then, that this educational question continues to be hotly debated, and consensus remains an impossible dream, both within individual educational institutions and between them?

In his masterful study of the idea of liberal education, Bruce Kimball analyzes the U.S. debate concerning postsecondary education in terms of the centuries-old debate between philosophers and orators.[34] The origins of the U.S. debate about what constitutes a proper education are situated in ancient Greece and Rome. Both orators and philosophers were committed to the formation of virtuous persons through the pursuit of knowledge, but they disagreed about the shape of the curriculum and the educational processes through which knowledge and virtue could be attained.

The philosophers, Plato and Socrates, argue that truth exists and can be known in itself and, further, that such knowledge will produce virtuous persons. Truth and therefore virtue can only be achieved through sustained inquiry and contemplation. For the philosophers, the highest form of education consists in the open-ended search for truth, beauty, and goodness through the study of the liberal arts, especially the sciences and philosophy. Clearly, not every person in Plato's aristocratic society enjoyed the leisure for such an educational pursuit. But the elite class of persons who did were responsible in this pursuit to the greater good of the whole society.

In contrast to the philosophers, the orators, including the Sophists and such individuals as Isocrates, Quintilian, and Cicero, argue that truth, beauty, and goodness cannot be pursued as abstract ideals, nor can the formation of virtuous persons depend on the contemplative activities of a few. Rather, they conclude that these virtues are discovered and taught through active engagement in the real life of society, which leads to the articulation of practical wisdom. The concerns of the orators are pragmatic. They commend the study of the liberal arts, stressing grammar and rhetoric over the sciences and philosophy, with the goal of defining truth in relation to particular contexts. Human behavior and virtues are shaped through the appropriation of received texts and traditions, which are re-presented through rhetorical means for practical ends. Here again, such learning is primarily available to persons with adequate wealth and leisure to participate, but its fruits are more immediately available to the larger society in which the orators practice their art.

The philosophers accuse the orators of sacrificing truth to mere rhetoric, of confining it to textual traditions, and of falsely imagining that virtuous persons could be formed through imitation and persuasion. The orators charge that the philosophers' commitment to open-ended, contemplative inquiry makes the truth unknowable and places the possibility of virtuous living beyond the reach of average citizens in a democratic society.

Even this brief sketch begins to make sense of the debates that continue to shape U.S. college and university education. The liberal arts tradition in the United States has been expressed in terms of education both as free inquiry (philosophers) and as the study of received textual traditions (orators). But in the U.S. context the classical debate undergoes some critical permutations. Kimball defines these permutations in terms of what he calls the "liberal free ideal."[35]

On the one side, the philosopher's commitment to free inquiry is eventually linked to scientific research methodologies dedicated to the objective pursuit of truth as empirical fact. Free inquiry is no longer grounded in philosophy and contemplation as the means to discover truth. Further, it ceases to be interested in the formation of persons who are virtuous in the classical sense—persons who understand and commit themselves to the virtues of truth, beauty, and goodness. The capacity for rational, critical, empirical inquiry becomes the key virtue to be formed in persons. On the other side, textual traditions that once provided examples of the virtues of truth, beauty, and goodness and formed students in the fine arts of logical thought and the rhetorical presentation of practical wisdom are now also submitted to the conventions of free critical inquiry. Texts are analyzed and criticized rather than imitated and appropriated. Virtuous persons do not submit to the authority and wisdom of received traditions—they question them.

The impact of the U.S. "liberal free ideal" on the classical liberal-arts ideals of the ancient philosophers and orators is far-reaching. Plato's epistemological assumption—that truth as an independently existing reality can be known through open-ended contemplative inquiry—is replaced by an assumption that the only truth that can be known is empirically verifiable truth. The dogmatic epistemology of the orators—that truth can be known through the study and comprehension of traditions—is replaced by an assumption that the truth of traditions must be questioned by each new generation. In both instances, it becomes less clear how human virtues will be broadly defined and formed in persons or whether education is even obliged to enable such formation.

I offer no judgment concerning these epistemological and ontological shifts, but rather intend to frame the complexity of the questions that surround U.S. college and university education. Assertions that the best postsecondary education is achieved through the liberal arts tradition must take into account that in the U.S. context precisely what this means for both the content of the curriculum and the processes of teaching and learning is immersed in muddy waters. It doesn't mean just one thing now, and in fact it never did.

There are voices calling for a return to the classical values of a liberal arts education. Howard Gardner has argued passionately for a return to education grounded in the formation of persons in the virtues of truth, beauty, and goodness.[36] His proposal echoes the oratorical strand of the liberal arts traditions, in which teaching and learning are based on the study of the best examples of these virtues that culture has to offer. Through such an education, persons will be able to distinguish between truth and falsehood, beauty and ugliness, good and evil. Gardner recognizes that the identification of the best examples of these virtues is complicated by the multicultural reality of American society, but he insists that such choices can and must be made for the sake of forming virtuous persons. Mortimer Adler is another outspoken advocate for a liberal arts education. He asserts that liberal learning is that which is not vocational, going so far as to claim that "it is an absolute misuse of school to include any vocational training at all."[37]

What Adler overlooks in making this assertion is that, from the outset, an education in the liberal arts was a vocational education: it prepared philosophers and orators in service to the greater social good. One might argue that these vocations are among the most noble and essential in society, but they are, nevertheless, vocations. Of course, Adler's concern is to speak against utilitarian and pragmatic traditions in U.S. higher education in favor of learning for its own sake. As we saw in chapter 3, in the U.S. context education for agrarian and industrial vocations existed alongside and outside colleges and universities focused on the preparation of persons for the learned and genteel vocations of ministry, law, and medicine. This separation began to shift with the Morrill Land Grant Acts of 1862 and 1890. Driven by the demands of an agrarian economy and growing industrialization, this legislation "supported postsecondary institutions for teaching 'agriculture and the mechanic arts'" and ultimately "introduced more practical, technical, and vocational subjects" into the mainstream of American higher education.[38] The distinct aims of liberal learning and preparation for a broad spectrum of practical vocations have been uneasy bedfellows for decades in America.

The utilitarian voices in American higher education might appeal to the philosophical tradition of pragmatism in support of their claims. John Dewey was responsible for most fully articulating the implications of pragmatism for education in a democracy. Arguing that social efficiency is among the chief aims of education, Dewey believed that no person could live without means of subsistence and that an individual who was not able to earn a living was "a drag or parasite upon the activities of others." According to Dewey, among other things, education must prepare persons for a vocation and equip them with the ability to make their way economically in the world.[39]

If this were the full extent of Dewey's philosophy of education, one might conclude that the newer voices in the debate over a proper college education find their support in this educational giant. Speaking from Wall Street and the socioeconomic concerns of industry and the marketplace are persons like Gregory Cappelli, a senior industry analyst at Credit Suisse First Boston, Michael Goldstein, head of institutions practice at Dow, Lohnes & Albertson in Washington, D.C., and Jeffrey Kittay, editor-in-chief of *University Business* magazine. They promote the utilitarian value of a college education for individual earning power, national productivity, and international competition, and they urge the influx of private investment capital into education in the interests of accountability and market responsiveness.

But Dewey's program of education for social efficiency goes beyond individual economic empowerment and vocational training. Dewey understood the human vocation in broad terms, as a vocation to participate fully in society in multiple roles with varying responsibilities.

Education must prepare persons to be good citizens, to exercise sound judgment about economic and social principles, to be adaptable in the face of rapid changes, to be flexible thinkers, and to participate in the transformation of social rules and norms. In the context of democracy, the principal aim of education is to inculcate a capacity among democratic citizens to communicate with one another, to continually work toward the development of shared values and common goals that will enable the smooth functioning and growth of the whole society and its individual members. In keeping with the oratorical strand of the liberal arts tradition, Dewey was convinced that education must prepare all persons to engage in persuasive rhetoric, not primarily for the purpose of persuading another to change perspective, but with the goal of creating understanding between a diversity of persons making choices and expressing values on the basis of their own best rationality.

Indeed, the purpose of higher education is a complex question. We are the inheritors of diverse philosophies, multiple educational traditions, and varying practices, a handful of which I have sketched above. Our assumptions about the nature and purpose of knowledge, the processes of knowing, the meaning of human existence, and the aims of society inform our choices about the content and practices of education.

With this book, I have attempted to describe the assumptions, content, and practices of for-profit institutions of higher education. I have argued that there may be opportunities for non-profit educational institutions to examine their own assumptions and practices in light of these new ventures in higher education. But I am also clear that the for-profits are not getting it right at every point. There are losses and gains in these ventures. Non-profit colleges and universities continue to hold in trust certain age-old educational values and remind us that some of the key benefits of education are simply not immediately measurable as outcomes, economic or otherwise. It is my intention to contribute to the ongoing conversation about higher education in America and to submit my own understanding and experience to the larger community of persons who also dedicate themselves to the human vocation of knowing and sharing knowledge, for the good of individuals and the larger society.

Notes

1 Confessions of a For-Profit Dean

1. J. Bear, "Diploma Mills," *University Business,* March 2000, 36.

2. The story of the early history of the University of Phoenix was told by President Jorge de Alva at a session entitled "For-Profit and Non-Profit Higher Education" at the annual conference of the Council for Higher Education Accreditation, Washington, D.C., 26 January 2000.

3. All of the numerical data presented here on the for-profit, degree-granting institutions are based on the National Center for Education Statistics, Integrated Postsecondary Education Data System (IPEDS) reports, available at *http://nces. ed.gov/index.html.* I relied particularly on the "Fall Enrollment 1996" survey. The estimate of 750 for-profit campuses in 2000 is my own, based on projections from the IPEDS data.

4. Charles E. M. Kolb, "Accountability in Postsecondary Education," in *Financing Postsecondary Education: The Federal Role—October, 1995* (U.S. Department of Education, 1995), 1, available at *http://www.ed.gov/offices/OPE/PPI/FinPostSecEd/ kolb.html.*

5. Ibid.

6. A. Krueger and S. Dale, "Estimating the Payoff to Attending a More Selective College: An Application of Selection on Observables and Unobservables,"

working paper W7289, National Bureau of Economic Research, August 1999. For a general overview of these kinds of studies, see B. Gose, "Measuring the Value of an Ivy Degree," *Chronicle of Higher Education,* 14 January 2000, A52–53.

7. John E. Sites, interview by author, Chicago, 31 March 2000.

8. See, for example, L. Lee, "Community Colleges and Proprietary Schools," *ERIC Digest,* September 1996, available at *http://www.ed.gov/databases/ERIC.*

9. D. Clowes and E. Hawthorne, eds., *Community Colleges and Proprietary Schools: Conflict or Convergence?* (Jossey-Bass, 1995), 19.

10. Sites, interview.

11. See K. Mangan, "For-profit Chains Don't Undercut Missions of Teaching Hospitals Study Finds," *Chronicle of Higher Education,* 17 March 2000, A42. The referenced study was conducted by David Blumenthal and Joel Weissman, of Harvard Medical School, and published in *Health Affairs,* March–April 2000).

12. B. Kimball, *Orators and Philosophers: A History of the Idea of Liberal Education,* expanded ed. (College Entrance Examination Board, 1995).

13. J. Pelikan, *The Idea of the University: A Reexamination* (Yale University Press, 1992); B. Readings, *The University in Ruins* (Harvard University Press, 1996); B. Wilshire, *The Moral Collapse of the University* (State University of New York Press, 1990); G. Nelson and S. Watt, *Academic Keywords: A Devil's Dictionary for Higher Education* (Routledge, 1999).

14. Milton Freeman's statements about *tax-paying* versus *tax-avoiding* appear in L. Spencer, "The Perils of Socialized Higher Education," *Forbes,* 27 May 1991, 294.

15. National Center for Education Statistics, *Digest of Educational Statistics* (1995), available at *http://nces.ed.gov/index.html.*

16. See M. Green, *Transforming Higher Education: Views from Leaders Around the World* (American Council on Higher Education, Oryx Press, 1997), 40–41.

17. Scott Cowen, "Leadership, Shared Governance, and the Change Imperative" (presentation at the Eighth American Association of Higher Education [AAHE] Conference on Faculty Roles and Rewards, New Orleans, La., 5 February 2000).

18. Ibid.

19. This view of liberal education is advanced by Mortimer J. Adler in *Reforming Education: The Opening of the American Mind* (Westview, 1977), 96–116.

20. "Why Is Research the Rule? The Impact of Incentive Systems on Faculty Behavior," The Landscape, *Change,* March–April 2000, 56.

21. Jorge de Alva, "Remaking the Academy in the Age of Information," *Issues in Science and Technology* 16 (winter 1999–2000): 54.

22. James Traub, "Drive-Thru U: Higher Education for People Who Mean Business," *New Yorker,* 20 and 27 October 1977.

2 The Players

1. R. Phipps et al., *Students at Private, For-Profit Institutions,* U.S. Department of Education, National Center for Education Statistics, Postsecondary Education Descriptive Analysis Report NCES 2000-175 (November 1999).

2. L. Horn and D. Carroll, *Nontraditional Undergraduates: Trends in Enroll-*

ment from 1986 to 1992 and Persistence and Attainment among 1989–90 Beginning Postsecondary Students, U.S. Department of Education, National Center for Education Statistics, Statistical Analysis Report NCES 97-578 (November 1996).

3. Ibid., 55. All of the NCES data reported here are from this report, pp. 51–55.

4. "Proprietary Preference: For-Profit Colleges Gain Momentum in Producing Graduates of Color," *Black Issues in Higher Education* 15 (9 July 1998): 30.

5. S. Choy and L. Bobbitt, *Low-Income Students: Who They Are and How They Pay for Their Education,* U.S. Department of Education, National Center for Higher Education Statistics, Statistical Analysis Report NCES 2000-169 (2000).

6. All of the quoted statements from president Stacey Sauchek were obtained during an interview by the author at the campus of the Art Institute of Philadelphia, 17 February 2000.

7. Michael Markovitz, "Letter to Our Shareholders," in the *Argosy Education Group, Inc., Annual Report, 1999* (December 1999), 4.

8. All of the comments by Eli Schwartz were obtained during an interview by the author, Chicago, 31 March 2000.

9. G. Blumenstyk, "Turning a Profit by Turning Out Professionals," *Chronicle of Higher Education,* 7 January 2000, A46.

10. John Shufold, interview by author, White Marsh, Md., 24 March 2000.

11. Harry Wilkins, interview by author, Jessup, Md., 24 March 2000.

12. Arthur Padilla, "The University of Phoenix, Inc.," *On the Horizon* 7 (July–August 1999). For other informative essays about the University of Phoenix, I recommend D. Stamps, "The For-Profit Future of Higher Education," *Training,* August 1988, 23–30; James Traub, "Drive-Thru U: Higher Education for People Who Mean Business," *New Yorker,* 20 and 27 October 1977; and M. Fischetti et al., "Education?" *University Business,* March–April 1998, 45–51. Also of interest is J. Sperling and R. W. Tucker, *For-Profit Higher Education: Developing a World-Class Workforce* (Transaction, 1997).

13. Fischetti et al., "Education?" 47.

14. Sperling and Tucker, *For-Profit Higher Education,* 51.

15. Padilla, "University of Phoenix, Inc.," 6.

16. Fischetti et al., "Education?" 50.

17. All of the quotations in this section from Jorge de Alva are from his presentation entitled "For-Profit and Non-Profit Higher Education," at the annual conference of the Council for Higher Education Accreditation, Washington, D.C., 26 January 2000.

18. Sperling and Tucker, *For-Profit Higher Education,* 1.

3 The History of For-Profit Education in the United States

1. C. M. Woodward, *The Manual Training School* (D. C. Heath & Co., 1887), 244, reprinted in the series American Education; Its Men, Ideas, and Institutions, ed. N. M. Butler (Arno Press and New York Times, 1969). This series provides source data on the early development of education in the United States. I relied heavily on these studies in tracing the origins of for-profit higher education. The quotation from the *Boston Transcript* is also reported by Woodward.

2. Ibid., 245.

3. Robert F. Seybolt, *The Evening School in Colonial America* (University of Illinois, Urbana, Bureau of Educational Research, 1925), 9, reprinted in the series American Education: Its Men, Ideas, and Institutions, ed. N. M. Butler (Arno Press and New York Times, 1969).

4. Robert F. Seybolt, *Source Studies in American Colonial Education: The Private School* (University of Illinois, Urbana, Bureau of Educational Research, 1925), 100, reprinted in the series American Education: Its Men, Ideas, and Institutions, ed. N. M. Butler (Arno Press and New York Times, 1969).

5. Ibid., 9–34. French was considered "polite and necessary." Italian was taught in New York City as early as 1755. Spanish and Portuguese were especially important to the large trade with the West Indies and South America.

6. Lawrence A. Cremin, *American Education: The Colonial Experience, 1607–1783* (Harper & Row, 1970). The companion volume is *American Education: The National Experience, 1783–1876* (Harper & Row, 1980).

7. Cremin, *American Education: The Colonial Experience,* 266, 401.

8. A. H. Smyth, "Observations Relative to the Intentions of the Original Founders of the Academy in Philadelphia," in *The Writings of Benjamin Franklin,* ed. Smyth, 10 vols. (Macmillan, 1905–7), 10:30, cited in Cremin, *American Education: The Colonial Experience,* 403.

9. Seybolt, *Source Studies in American Education,* 35.

10. Cremin, *American Education: The Colonial Experience,* 375.

11. For several examples of the interweaving of church and state, see M. O'Neill, *The Third America: The Emergence of the Non-Profit Sector in the United States* (Jossey-Bass, 1989), 24.

12. Ibid., 24, 54–55.

13. Cremin, *American Education: The Colonial Experience,* 178.

14. A. C. Bolino, *Career Education: Contributions to Economic Growth* (Praeger, 1973), 18–23. This book traces the history and development of private career schools in America up to the early 1970s.

15. Ibid., 21.

16. Ibid., 22–25. See also C. A. Anderson and M. J. Bowman, eds., *Education and Economic Development* (Aldine, 1965), 137.

17. Edmund J. James, "Commercial Education," in *Monographs on Education in the United States,* ed. N. M. Butler, Department of Education for the United States Commission to the Paris Exposition of 1900 (J. B. Lyon, 1900), 5, reprinted in the series American Education: its Men, Ideas, and Institutions, ed. N. M. Butler (Arno Press and New York Times, 1969).

18. Cremin, *American Education: The National Experience,* 276–78.

19. The perceived political need to secure a small social elite against the rising popularity of Jacksonian egalitarianism is well documented. See L. Vesey, "Stability and Experiment in the American Undergraduate Curriculum," in *Content and Context: Essays on College Education, A Report Prepared for the Carnegie Commission on Higher Education,* ed. C. Kaysen (McGraw-Hill, 1973), 2–10.

20. Cremin, *American Education: The Colonial Experience,* 397.

21. Charles W. Dabney, "Agricultural Education," in Butler, *Monographs on Education in the United States*, 602.

22. Bolino, *Career Education*, 39.

23. Ibid., 606.

24. Ibid., 606.

25. For several examples see Butler, *Monographs on Education in the United States*.

26. Cremin, *American Education: The National Experience*, 219.

27. Ibid., 218–45.

28. See Robert F. Seybolt, "The Education of Girls in Colonial America," in *Source Studies in American Colonial Education*, 69–82.

29. Ibid., 72.

30. Booker T. Washington, "Education of the Negro," in Butler, *Monographs on Education in the United States*, 895–936.

31. Cremin, *American Education: The National Experience*, 235–38.

32. Ibid., 239.

33. W. N. Hailmann, "Education of the Indian," in Butler, *Monographs on Education in the United States*, 939–72.

34. E. E. Allen, "Education of Defectives," in ibid., 771–819.

35. Seybolt, *Evening Schools in Colonial America*, 59.

36. See, for example, the series American Education: Its Men, Ideas, and Institutions, ed. N. M. Butler.

37. M. P. Garber, "Wall Street Ph.D.," *National Review*, 30 September 1996, 57.

38. S. Barbett and R. A. Korb, "Current Funds Revenues and Expenditures of Degree-Granting Institutions: Fiscal Year 1996," U.S. Department of Education, National Center for Education Statistics, Integrated Postsecondary Education Data System Finance Survey, NCES Report 1999-161 (1999), 1.

39. Robert L. Craig, managing director, EVEREN Securities, Inc., interview in *The Wall Street Transcript: Special Focus, The Education Industry*, 26 April 1999, 28. Analysts at EVEREN have created an education industry index comprising 73 publicly traded companies, of which 16 are for-profit postsecondary institutions.

40. Merrill Lynch, *In-Depth Report: The Book of Knowledge, Investing in the Growing Education and Training Industry*, Report 1268 (9 April 1999), 5.

41. Jerry R. Herman, managing director, EVEREN Securities, Inc., interview in *Wall Street Transcript: Special Focus*, 31.

42. Gary Kerber, interview by Bill Griffeth, anchor of CNBC Power Lunch, 26 May 1999, transcribed from CNBC/Dow Jones Business Video, *Power Lunch, Quest Education, Chairman and CEO Interview (May 26, 1999)*.

43. Quest Education Corporation, *Annual Report* (June 29, 1999), 4, available at *www.edgar-online.com*.

44. Corinthian Schools, Inc., press release, 4 April 2000, available at *www.biz.yahoo.com/prnews*.

45. See J. M. McLaughlin, ed., *The Education Industry Report: News and Commentary on the Education Industry* (The Education Industry Group, July 1999), available at *www.edindustry.com*.

46. This prediction of 25 percent of the market is my own.

47. Michael Heise, quoted in Garber, "Wall Street Ph.D."

48. See, for example, D. Gross, "Not for Profit? Not Exactly," *University Business,* April 1999, 31–36.

49. James Duderstadt, "Revolutionary Changes: Understanding the Challenges and the Possibilities," *Business Officer* (National Association of College and University Business Officers) July 1997, 7, available at *www.nacubo.org.*

50. For a comprehensive discussion of the business of higher education from the perspective of leading industry analysts, see *Wall Street Transcript: Special Focus.*

51. See M. Ankrum, "Roundtable Forum on the Education Industry," in ibid., 13.

52. Ibid., 20.

53. G. W. Cappelli, "Roundtable Forum on the Education Industry," in *Wall Street Transcript: Special Focus,* 4.

54. J. Sperling and R. W. Tucker, *For-Profit Higher Education: Developing a World-Class Workforce* (Transaction, 1997), 2.

55. James Traub, "Drive-Thru U: Higher Education for People Who Mean Business," *New Yorker,* 20 and 27 October 1997.

56. J. Ruark, "Venerable College Board Announces For-Profit Internet Venture," *Chronicle of Higher Education,* 27 September 1999, available at *www.chronicle.com/daily.*

57. Edward O'Neil, quoted in "Not-So-Distant Competitors: Readers React," *AAHE Bulletin* (May 1998), available at *www.aahe.org/bulletin.*

58. Scott Cowen, "Role Models for a Changing World," *The Presidency* 2 (spring 1999): 24.

59. "Proprietary Preference: For-Profit Colleges Gain Momentum in Producing Graduates of Color," *Black Issues in Higher Education* 15 (9 July 1998): 30.

60. Claude M. Steele, "Race and the Schooling of Black Americans," *Atlantic Monthly,* April 1992; idem, "Thin Ice: 'Stereotype Threat' and Black College Students," ibid., August 1999.

61. These quotations from students were presented at "Dealing with the Invisible Barriers in the Classroom," a DeVry faculty symposium held in Red Bank, New Jersey, on 22 October 1999.

62. See M. Soliday, "Symposium: English 1999, Class Dismissed," *College English* 61 (July 1999).

4 The Financing of For-Profit Higher Education

1. For a discussion of the economic theory and econometric modeling in higher-education financing, see D. S. P. Hopkins and W. F. Massy, *Planning Models for Colleges and Universities* (Stanford University Press, 1981); and W. F. Massy, ed., *Resource Allocation in Higher Education* (University of Michigan Press, 1996).

2. Robert L. Lenington, *Managing Higher Education as a Business* (American Council on Education, Oryx Press, 1996), x.

3. Peter T. Ewell, "Imitation as Art: Borrowed Management Techniques in Higher Education," *Change,* November–December 1999, 15.

4. Daniel J. Julius, "Case Studies from the Floor: Getting Down to Brass Tacks" (presentation at the "Market-Driven Higher Education" conference, hosted by *University Business* magazine, New York City, 7 October 1999).

5. Ewell, "Imitation as Art," 14–15.

6. Ibid., 15.

7. See G. W. Cappelli, "Post-Secondary Education Stocks," in *Wall Street Transcript, Analyst Interview,* 15 November 1999, 2.

8. Ibid., 2–4.

9. M. Van Der Werf, "The Precarious Balancing Act of Small Liberal Arts Colleges," *Chronicle of Higher Education,* 30 July 1999, A32–33.

10. D. J. Julius, J. V. Baldridge, and J. Pfeffer, "A Memo from Machiavelli," *Journal of Higher Education,* March–April 1999.

11. D. Franecki, "Matters of Degree," *Wall Street Journal,* 29 November 1999, R17.

12. Mathew Miller, "$140,000—And a Bargain," *New York Times Magazine,* 13 June 1999, 48–49.

13. Ibid., 49.

14. For an analysis of the lack of adequate costing practices in traditional higher education, see Lenington, *Managing Higher Education as a Business,* 56–66.

15. J. F. Carlin, "Restoring Sanity to an Academic World Gone Mad," *Chronicle of Higher Education,* 5 November 1999, A76.

16. Frederick E. Balderston, *Managing Today's University: Strategies for Viability, Change, and Excellence,* 2nd ed. (Jossey-Bass, 1995), 155.

17. Mark Da Cunha, "Profit," *www.capitalism.org.*

18. Lenington, *Managing Higher Education as a Business,* 164.

19. B. Gose, "Surge in Continuing Education Brings Profits for Universities," *Chronicle of Higher Education,* 19 February 1999.

20. See the interview with Milton Friedman in L. Spencer, "The Perils of Socialized Higher Education," *Forbes,* 27 May 1991, 294.

21. Lenington, *Managing Higher Education as a Business,* 8.

22. Balderston, *Managing Today's University,* 163.

23. Charles E. M. Kolb, "Accountability in Postsecondary Education," in *Financing Postsecondary Education: The Federal Role—October 1995* (U.S. Department of Education, 1995), available at *www.ed.gov/offices/OPE/PPI/FinPostSecEd.*

24. Benno C. Schmidt Jr., "The View from Both Sides of the Fence" (presentation at the "Market-Driven Higher Education" conference, hosted by *University Business* magazine, New York City, 7 October 1999). Additional parts of his story were provided during an informal conversation with the author on the same date.

25. Ibid.

26. Merrill Lynch, *In-Depth Report: The Book of Knowledge, Investing in the Growing Education and Training Industry,* Report 1268 (9 April 1999), 65.

27. Howard Gardner, *The Disciplined Mind: What Every Student Should Understand* (Simon & Schuster, 1999), 15–22.

28. Annual Report, Educational Management Corporation, 26, available at *www.biz.yahoo.com/edmc.*

29. The annual *Almanac* edition of the *Chronicle of Higher Education* provides comparative data on the relationship between the rate of inflation and the price of tuition. For an interesting commentary see Miller, "$140,000—And a Bargain."

30. William W. Jellema, *From Red to Black?* (Jossey-Bass, 1973), 88–138.

31. Company financial statements, summarized in Smith Barney, *Education Industry: Investments for a Knowledge-Based Economy,* equity research report SF05E162 (May 1997).

32. Jellema, *From Red to Black?* 124.

33. Smith Barney, *Education Industry,* 42–123.

34. A number of investment houses, notably Merrill Lynch, Banc of America, and Smith Barney, have reported figures in this range. The figures quoted here are from a presentation by Michael Eleey, of Communications Equity Associates, at the "Market-Driven Higher Education" conference, hosted by *University Business* magazine, New York City, 7 October 1999.

35. Smith Barney, *Education Industry,* 1.

36. For a more detailed analysis of Apollo's new campus start-up strategies, see H. Block, ed., *The E-Bang Theory,* Illuminoso Volume 2, Banc of America Securities, Education Industry Overview (September 1999), 165–76.

37. Ibid., 172.

38. D. Goodwin, *Beyond Defaults: Indicators of Accessing Proprietary School Quality* (report prepared for the U.S. Department of Education, Planning and Evaluation Service, Office of the Under Secretary, August 1991), 3. See also M. A. Schenet, *Proprietary Schools: The Regulatory Structure* (Congressional Research Service, Library of Congress, 31 August 1990).

39. Ibid., 16.

5 The Academic Culture of For-Profit Universities

1. Jonathan Fife, introduction to *Proprietary Schools: Programs, Policies, and Prospects,* by J. B. Lee and J. P. Merisotis, ASHE-ERIC Higher Education Report No. 5 (George Washington University, 1990).

2. Edmund J. James, "Commercial Education," in *Monographs on Education in the United States,* ed. N. M. Butler, Department of Education for the United States Commission to the Paris Exposition of 1900 (J. B. Lyon, 1900), 657, 661.

3. Educational Policies Commission of the National Educational Association and the American Association of School Administrators, *The Structure and Administration of Education in American Democracy* (1938), 23, reported in J. W. Miller, *A Critical Analysis of the Organization, Administration, and Function of the Private Business Schools of the United States* (South-Western, 1938), 4.

4. H. A. Tonne, "Private Schools Not a Phase of Our Educational System," *Journal of Business Education* 14 (November 1938): 7.

5. Scott Cowen, "Leadership, Shared Governance, and the Change Imperative" (presentation at the Eighth AAHE Conference on Faculty Roles and Rewards, New Orleans, La., 5 February 2000).

6. W. H. Bergquest, *The Four Cultures of the Academy* (Jossey-Bass, 1992). Of the four basic types in Bergquest's scheme—collegial, managerial, developmental,

and negotiating—the managerial type comes the closest to describing the culture of the for-profits.

7. See James Duderstadt, "Revolutionary Changes: Understanding the Challenges and the Possibilities," *Business Officer* (National Association of College and University Business Officers), July 1997, 8, available at *www.nacubo.org*.

8. Eli Schwartz, interview by author, Chicago, 31 March 2000.

9. See the current business profile of the Apollo Group, Inc., including quarterly and annual reports, at *http://biz.yahoo.com*.

10. An academic dean at one of the for-profits, conversation with author, December 1999.

11. James S. Coleman, "The University and Society's New Demands Upon It," in *Content and Context: Essays on College Education, A Report Prepared for the Carnegie Commission on Higher Education,* ed. C. Kaysen (McGraw-Hill, 1973), 397.

12. Academic dean at one of the for-profits, conversation with author, December 1999.

13. Peter C. Magrath, "Eliminating Tenure Without Destroying Academic Freedom," *Chronicle of Higher Education,* 28 February 1997, A60.

14. Richard Chait, "The Future of Tenure," *AGB Priorities* 1 (spring 1995); idem, "New Pathways: Faculty Careers and Employment in the 21st Century," AAHE, New Pathways Working Paper Series (March 1997); idem, "Rethinking Tenure: Toward New Templates for Academic Employment," *Harvard Magazine,* July–August 1997.

15. Lennard Davis, "The Uses of Fear and Envy in Academe," *Chronicle of Higher Education,* 11 June 1999, B8.

16. The proposition that the real problem with tenure is bad hiring decisions in the first place has recently been articulated by C. Nelson and S. Watt in *Academic Keywords: A Devil's Dictionary for Higher Education* (Routledge, 1999), 298.

17. "Academic Freedom," *New York Times,* Sunday, 15 June 1915, 1.

18. A. B. Wolfe, "The Graduate School, Faculty Responsibility, and the Training of University Teachers," *School and Society* 4, no. 90 (1916): 4.

19. See P. G. Altbach, "Harsh Realities: The Professorate Faces a New Century," in *American Higher Education in the 21st Century,* ed. P. G. Altbach et al. (Johns Hopkins University Press, 1999), 289.

20. American Association of University Professors, *Policy Documents and Reports* (1995), 3–10.

21. For a discussion of the modern university's loss of its communal identity, see Coleman, "The University and Society's New Demands Upon It."

22. *Academic Policy Manual,* DeVry, Inc., effective 9 March 1998.

23. Ibid.

24. Many studies of grade inflation apparently bear similar results. See T. Sowell, "A Gentleman's 'A,'" *Forbes,* 4 July 1994, 82.

25. Rider University administrator, conversation with author, 26 July 1999.

26. See E. Watson, "College Grade Inflation Getting Out of Hand," *Headway* 9 (May 1997): 27.

27. Information on the Noel-Levitz Student Satisfaction Inventory is available at *www.info@noellevitz.com.*

6 Lessons from the For-Profit Side

1. G. Keller, "The Emerging Third State in Higher Education Planning," *Planning for Higher Education* 28 (winter 1999–2000): 3.

2. National Center for Education Statistics, "Education and the Economy: An Indicators Report," NCES 97-939 (March 1997), available at *www.nces.ed.gov. pubs97.*

3. Ibid., 4–5.

4. These figures are projections based on the IPEDS "Fall Enrollment 1996" survey.

5. G. Blumenstyk, "Turning a Profit by Turning Out Professionals," *Chronicle of Higher Education,* 7 January 2000, A46.

6. "The American Freshman: National Norms for the Fall 1999," Higher Education Research Institute, University of California at Los Angeles, Graduate School of Education and Information Studies, available at *www.gseis.ucla.edu/heri/heri/ html.* The results mentioned were summarized in the *Chronicle of Higher Education,* 28 January 2000, A49–52.

7. For a general overview of these kinds of studies, see B. Gose, "Measuring the Value of an Ivy Degree," *Chronicle of Higher Education,* 14 January 2000, A52–53.

8. A. Krueger and S. Dale, "Estimating the Payoff to Attending a More Selective College: An Application of Selection on Observables and Unobservables," working paper W7289, National Bureau of Economic Research, August 1999.

9. Roseann Runte, "How to Succeed in Academe: A Question of Degrees," *Chronicle of Higher Education,* 8 January 2000, B8.

10. Jorge de Alva, "For-Profit and Non-Profit Higher Education" (presentation at the annual conference of the Council for Higher Education Accreditation, Washington, D.C., 26 January 2000).

11. Judith Eaton, *Core Academic Values, Quality, and Regional Accreditation: The Challenge of Distance Learning,* CHEA Monograph Series 2000, 1.

12. Ibid.

13. Patricia McGuire, "For-Profit and Non-Profit Higher Education" (presentation at the annual conference of the Council for Higher Education Accreditation, Washington, D.C., 26 January 2000).

14. See A. McGuinness Jr., "The States and Higher Education," in *Higher Education in the 21st Century,* ed. P. G. Altbach et al. (Johns Hopkins University Press, 1999), 183–84.

15. Zachary Karabell, *What's College For? The Struggle to Define American Higher Education* (Basic Books, 1998), 237.

16. De Alva, "For-Profit and Non-Profit Higher Education."

17. John Sperling, quoted in D. Stamps, "The For-Profit Future of Higher Education," *Training,* August 1998, 25.

18. Karabell, *What's College For?* xi.

19. Ibid., x.

20. See, for example, P. G. Altbach, "Harsh Realities: The Professorate Faces a New Century," in Altbach et al., *American Higher Education in the 21st Century;* and Frederick E. Balderston, *Managing Today's University: Strategies for Viability, Change, and Excellence,* 2nd ed. (Jossey-Bass, 1995).

21. McGuinness, "The States and Higher Education," 183.

22. William Tierney, *Building the Responsive Campus: Creating High Performance Colleges and Universities* (Sage, 1999), 75–97.

23. Patricia Gumport and Marc Chun, "Technology in Higher Education," in Altbach et al., *American Higher Education in the 21st Century,* 389.

24. Scott Cowen, "Leadership, Shared Governance, and the Change Imperative" (presentation at the Eighth AAHE Conference on Faculty Roles and Rewards, New Orleans, La., 5 February 2000).

25. R. Geiger, "The Ten Generations of American Higher Education," in Altbach et al., *American Higher Education in the 21st Century,* 64.

26. Jorge de Alva, "Remaking the Academy in the Age of Information," *Issues in Science and Technology* 16 (winter 1999–2000): 52.

27. These market-share penetration figures were reported by Merrill Lynch in *In-Depth Report: The Book of Knowledge, Investing in the Growing Education and Training Industry,* Report 1268 (9 April 1999), 44. The figures originally appeared in a study by the Miliken Institute.

28. Michael McPherson, "Balancing Competing Values: The Market and the Mission," *The Presidency* 2 (spring 1999): 27.

29. Merrill Lynch, *In-Depth Report,* 49.

30. Michael B. Goldstein, head of the Educational Institutions, Public Policy, and Government Relations practice at Dow, Lohnes & Albertson, Washington, D.C., interview by author, 25 January 2000.

31. Daniel Julius, "Case Studies from the Floor: Getting Down to Brass Tacks" (presentation at the "Market-Driven Higher Education" conference, hosted by *University Business* magazine, New York City, 7 October 1999).

32. Ibid.

33. For invaluable help in framing this analysis I am indebted to Renee S. House, "The Inevitable Richness of Knowing" (doctoral seminar paper, Princeton Theological Seminary, fall 1999).

34. B. Kimball, *Orators and Philosophers: A History of the Idea of Liberal Education,* expanded ed. (College Entrance Examination Board, 1995).

35. Ibid., ch. 5.

36. Howard Gardner, *The Disciplined Mind: What All Students Should Understand* (Simon & Schuster, 1999).

37. Mortimer J. Adler, *Reforming Education: The Opening of the American Mind* (Westview, 1977), 103.

38. Kimball, *Orators and Philosophers,* 181.

39. J. Dewey, *Democracy and Education: An Introduction to the Philosophy of Education* (Macmillan, 1920), 139.

Index